DISA
IT Acquisition Guide

Proactively Tailored Acquisition Models and
Processes to Guide DISA's Acquisition of
IT Products and Services

1 November 2013

Version 1.0

DISA Acquisition Community,

Our vision is to foster a world-class acquisition organization using innovative and effective acquisition discipline to rapidly deliver best value capabilities for the Global Information Grid. In support of this vision, this guidebook provides a series of proactively tailored IT acquisition models to assist you in the effective acquisition of IT products and services. The traditional acquisition models in Department of Defense Instruction (DODI) 5000.02 have been customized and streamlined to account for the diverse set of IT capabilities DISA acquires. It provides guidance for each step of each model and the information required at the decision points. These models should be further tailored to meet the unique aspects of your program, project, or initiative. As each DISA organization acquires products and services differently, this guide will help provide a foundation for more common, repeatable processes, while allowing the flexibility to tailor based on mission needs.

My guiding principles for development and implementation of these models are:

- Streamlined, repeatable processes for rapid capability deliveries
- Acquisition rigor that is balanced with ease-of-use for acquisition experts and novices
- Tailored processes and documents based on size, complexity, and approvals
- Accommodates the unique aspects of the IT products and services DISA acquires
- Integrates the DISA specific organizations and processes (e.g. DITCO, JITC)
- Spans the entire acquisition lifecycle from initial requirement through sustainment

Future versions of this guidebook will provide additional details and will be updated based on implementation and your feedback. Please share your best practices and feedback on this guidebook so we can continue to improve our processes as an enterprise. You can provide your comments and feedback by emailing the Acquisition Support Center or by contacting them by phone at 304-225-4150.

Dr. Jennifer Carter
DISA Component Acquisition Executive

2

Table of Contents

3

Acknowledgments

This guidebook was created by the DISA Office of the Component Acquisition Executive (CAE), with the support of The MITRE Corporation. This guidebook was a collaborative effort that was made possible by contributions from the Program Executive Offices (PEOs), Directorates, and Strategic Business Units. All comments and feedback can be emailed to the Acquisition Support Center or by phone at 304-225-4150.

Chapter I   Introduction

The DISA IT Acquisition Framework includes nine proactively tailored IT acquisition models for DISA products and services. USD(AT&L), the Defense Acquisition Executive, stresses that the first responsibility of acquisition leaders is to think—by tailoring acquisition processes to fit their program. Managers should structure their programs and projects to effectively and efficiently deliver capabilities to the warfighters. This guide offers acquisition models that have been adapted from the traditional DoD 5000.02, Business Capability Lifecycle (BCL), and Acquisition of Services approaches. They provide customized approaches for DISA acquisition team leaders (program managers, project managers, and project leaders) focused on delivery of IT capabilities to the warfighter. DISA acquisition team leaders are encouraged to use these acquisition models to acquire any product or service and tailor further if necessary for the size, scope, complexity, or phase of acquisition.

The acquisition team that is referred to throughout this document is the team managing the program, project, service procurement, or related effort to acquire capabilities. It may include a program/project manager/leader, systems engineers, cost analysts, contracting personnel, testers, architects, and other acquisition professionals from across DISA. As shown in Figure 1, all acquisitions begin with an initiation phase, followed by a Decision Point 1 that determines which of the IT acquisition models to follow.

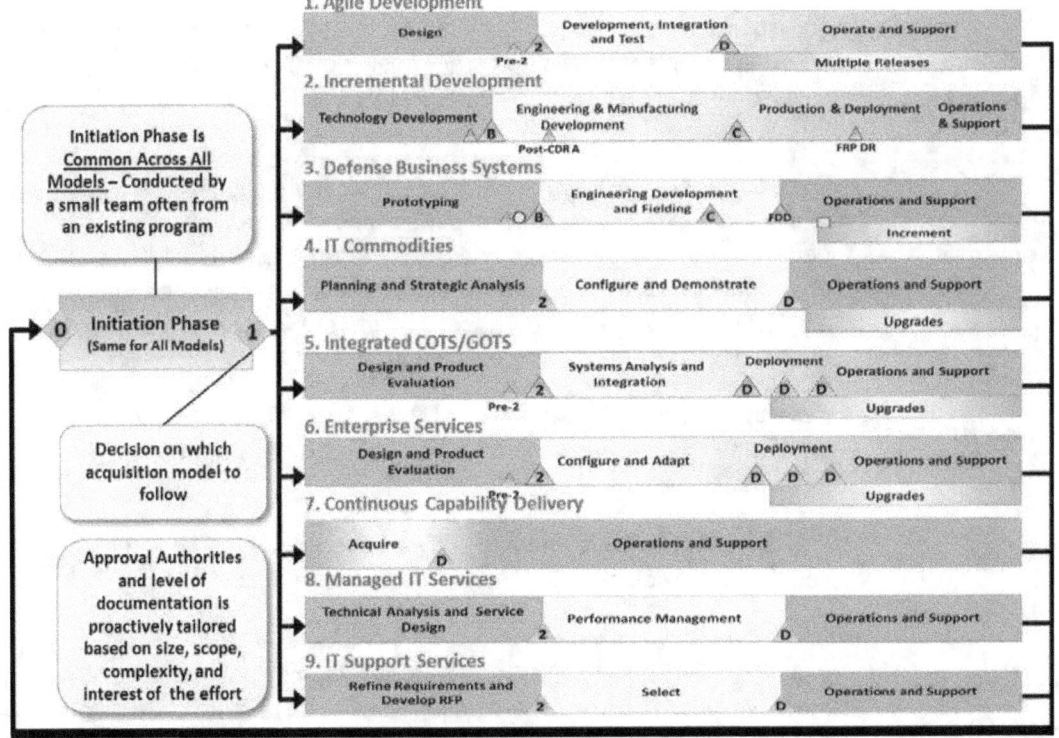

Figure 1 DISA IT Acquisition Framework

The acquisition models in Figure 1 identify decision authority review points as either a Milestone or Decision Point. Models 2 and 3 reference traditional Milestones (A, B, and C). These models are adapted from DoD 5000 and Business Capability Lifecycle (BCL). The remaining models refer to these junctures in the acquisition process generically as Decision Points.

DISA acquires a wide range of products and services that require a diverse set of acquisition processes. For example, the development of a new command and control software system is different from the acquisition of an enterprise service or the way that help desk support is obtained. Models 1 and 2 are software development models for the acquisition of DoD unique software applications. Models 3 through 7 are commercial-off-the-shelf (COTS) models that vary based on the type of acquisition, level of integration, and/or enterprise delivery. Models 8 and 9 support IT service acquisitions for an end-to-end managed IT capability and for professional IT support services, respectively. An IT capability may be acquired via multiple approaches, depending on constraints, risks, requirements, strategies, personnel, budgets, and other factors. The acquisition team should select the model that best fits the acquisition strategy, and the many inputs that shape it, as it is formulated in the initiation phase.

Table 1. DISA IT Acquisition Model Definitions

	IT Acquisition Model	Definition
Development	1. Agile Development	Development and/or customization of DoD unique software applications often via multiple releases, generally hosted on COTS or existing military hardware platform. The prime contractor is often responsible for integration.
	2. Incremental Development	Development of DoD unique hardware or software applications often via one or more larger increments of capabilities. Program often includes development of infrastructure and/or software. Appropriate for major programs for which the deployment and operational user community are significantly impacted by new capability delivery. Processes conform to the traditional DoD 5000 acquisition model.
COTS/GOTS	3. Defense Business Systems	Development or customization of COTS software for DoD business processes. Processes conform to the DoD Business Capability Lifecycle (BCL).
	4. IT Commodities	COTS and GOTS hardware and software products (non-development items) that provide needed functionality "out-of-the-box."
	5. Integrated COTS/GOTS	Integration of two or more COTS/GOTS products that are integrated into an existing system. New software development is minimized. This model includes IT Environment acquisitions (e.g., Infrastructure as a Service (IaaS) and Platform as a Service (PaaS)). DISA is responsible for overall systems integration.

6. Enterprise Services	Configuration, integration, and/or customization of COTS/GOTS products and services as a DISA enterprise service for DOD-wide use.
7. Continuous Capability Delivery	IT portfolios and programs that satisfy a long term capability requirement on a continuous basis. Focuses primarily on the activities that take place after Deployment and addresses the long term nature (10 years +) of functionally related IT solutions that are in the operations and sustainment mode.
8. Managed IT Services	Capitalizes on the benefits of managed services provided by an outside service or existing operational service provider. The contractor or service provider is the systems integrator, owns hardware/software, and manages configuration. DISA does not own any infrastructure and systems integration responsibilities.
9. IT Support Services	IT support services provides DISA operational capability such as help desk, network management, program support services, transport services and operating equipment & facilities.

1 Purpose/How to Use This Guidebook

This guidebook provides details for acquisition models tailored to optimize capability delivery for the types of IT acquisition that enable DISA's mission. The purpose of these models is to build agility into the acquisition process by defining a baseline that enables rapid delivery of DISA IT products, services, and capabilities. The acquisition team and Decision Authority (DA) can further tailor the processes, documents, and reviews as necessary to effectively and efficiently deliver IT capabilities to the warfighter. Tailoring considerations include system complexity, detail of system definition, constraints and requirements, technology base, risks, level of documentation, and organizational best practices. Tailoring must be implemented with the intent of preserving the requirements traceability, baseline control, lifecycle focus, maturity tracking, and integration inherent in an acquisition approach.

Every acquisition starts with an initiation phase for which the intended outcome is to support a program initiation decision and to establish an executable program baseline. Each of the DISA acquisition models has its own section in Chapter III to guide the acquisition team through the acquisition processes. The acquisition processes described in Chapter III reference procedures and special considerations specific to each model. Some models also contain model variations with descriptions of how the process steps differ for each variation. Chapter IV provides a description of common processes that cut across several of the acquisition models. Related reference materials can be found on the CAE website, and for convenience this guidebook contains hyperlinks to internal and external sources for related additional guidance, templates, and policies.

Throughout the guidebook, a series of questions are captured in blue boxes. These questions are designed to *help acquisition team leaders think critically about what is required for key acquisition processes* within the acquisition model. Decision Authorities will use these questions during milestone and Decision Point reviews to ensure that proper considerations have been made during key planning phases of the acquisition. The green boxes throughout the guidebook identify the information

requirements that should be documented for milestone and Decision Point approvals. Decision Authorities will use Decision Points to verify that the acquisition is on track and key outcomes are being met. The acquisition team is encouraged to tailor the acquisition documentation as necessary to support effective and efficient delivery.

DoD 5000 identifies a set of required acquisition documents that vary based on the acquisition category (ACAT), product or service, and type of acquisition (e.g., Defense Business Systems). For each acquisition model, the documents listed in the "Information Required" green boxes are the minimum set of required documents to be in compliance with DoD 5000 requirements. However, each program can tailor the documentation requirements appropriately with a signed ADM specifying approval for the tailored list of milestone documentation requirements and rationale. Tailoring can include adding or streamlining documentation. For example, Major Automated Information Systems (MAIS) ACAT programs have an additional set of required documentation. Each program/project should check the full list of DoD 5000 documents and the conditions of applicability to ensure compliance with regulation. A list of the required acquisition documents has been provided in Appendix C of this guidebook.

This is version 1.0 of the guidebook, providing initial guidance on the acquisition models. This initial version also includes instructions for the initiation phase, as well as varying levels of detail for each of the acquisition models. Future versions of this guidebook will progressively build on the materials in this guide. The DISA acquisition community is encouraged to provide feedback on the guidebook and offer ideas on how to improve the information provided in this guide to ensure it reflects current and relevant DISA practices. Comments and feedback on the guide can be emailed to the Acquisition Support Center or by calling 304-225-4150.

2   Applicability

This guidebook is applicable to DISA acquisition programs, pilots, projects, and initiatives. Within an acquisition program or project, there may be several smaller efforts for sustainment and technical refresh. This guidebook provides guidance for the acquisition of all DISA IT products and services; however, acquisition team leaders are encouraged to use discretion when applying its processes and concepts. Ideally a program baseline is structured to support agile delivery of capability throughout the lifecycle, including periodic technology insertion that will improve existing capabilities in sustainment. In cases where the requirements are expanded, a program may need to be re-baselined, the need for which is dependent on the level of change. For instance, a routine upgrade to a fielded operational system does not require the program/project to revisit the initiation phase and execute a brand new acquisition. On the other hand, a major release that requires a change to the underlying system architecture may require the program to revisit the initiation phase and select a new acquisition model. Business systems are an exception to the direct applicability of these models; however, some of the same tailoring principles may apply. Business Systems are required to follow the current policy and guidelines for the Business Capability Lifecycle (BCL). Acquisition teams are given a wide range of flexibility to operate within this guidance to effectively deliver the IT products and services for the DoD.

3 Decision Authority

The Decision Authority is the individual with review and approval responsibility. The Decision Authority for services acquisition is defined in CAE Guideline Number 001. The Decision Authority for programs and projects are defined in DISA Instruction 610-22-5-2. The specific Decision Authority may vary from guidance based on documented MDA delegation decisions. Generally, decision authorities will review decision points via an Acquisition Review Board (ARB), which is covered under CAE Guideline Number 005. Each organization may have its own set of reviews leading up to an ARB, and additional engineering and/or operational boards may also be required (e.g., Chief Engineers Panel (CEP), Net Readiness Review Board (NRRB)). For acquisition projects that will impact DISA Operations, participation in the NetOps Readiness Review Process (NRRP) during the entire acquisition lifecycle is required to ensure operational considerations are integrated into planning, design, and development. The NRRB verifies completion of the NRRP and assesses residual operational risk prior to operational fielding. When planning an acquisition, the acquisition team should identify critical points in the process where these governance bodies can provide value to the acquisition. In some cases, this may take place outside of major decision points and milestones. DISA organizations should document in the acquisition strategy how these reviews are being leveraged, streamlined, and/or standardized as appropriate. For a description of each of the various review boards, see Chapter IV, Section 11.

4 Defense Enterprise Systems Management Framework

To improve its delivery of services, DISA is developing and implementing the Defense Enterprise Service Management Framework (DESMF), which is based on the Information Technology Infrastructure Library (ITIL) and other industry best-practices. The DESMF describes best practice processes for service design and transition to operations and sustainment. The processes and key questions that are included throughout this document are consistent with the DESMF.

The application of DESMF principles and processes is not confined to the operations and sustainment phases; it begins during the requirements definition, as services are being defined. In addition to the mission or business requirements, the DESMF processes for Service Level management, capacity, continuity and availability will establish additional requirements for the service. This will be true for either developed or acquired services. As the acquisition progresses beyond Decision Point 1 (Design, Development) the Asset, Configuration and Change Management processes will have important impacts on the definition of solutions and implementation plans. As the acquisition progresses beyond Decision Point 2, the Release and Deployment processes will inform the transition and operations and sustainment planning efforts. Operating and sustaining the delivery of services after the deployment decision brings the DESMF processes to bear assuring the continuous delivery of effective and efficient services to all customers.

Chapter II   Initiation Phase

The objectives of the initiation phase are to analyze and mature requirements, analyze potential alternatives and cost impacts, assess competition, develop a rough order of magnitude (ROM) cost estimate or contract ceiling, conduct market research, and develop an initial acquisition strategy based on the selection of one of the acquisition models. ***The initiation phase is common across all models*** and is conducted by a small team often from an existing program. As illustrated in Figure 2, as high-level requirements are received, the team assesses potential alternatives, formulates an initial strategy, and determines the best acquisition model to use. The schedule and level of effort for this phase will vary based on the size, complexity, risk, and approval of the program. At Decision Point 0, the Decision Authority will provide the team with guidance on the scope of the alternatives to explore. Some capabilities that have traditionally been managed as development efforts may now be more effectively acquired via a COTS product or services contract. As the team examines related programs and conducts market research, additional alternatives may emerge.

Based on DISA's key role as a DoD-level enterprise provider of IT capabilities, program initiation may include transitioning existing capabilities or programs from external sources and re-baselining them as a DISA program or enterprise service offering. For this type of program, the initiation phase is modified to focus on assessment of the existing requirement, program baseline, and capability. Similar to the outcome of the initiation phase for a new program, this program transition assessment supports not only making a transition decision but also transition planning and establishing the appropriate program baseline (cost, schedule, performance, organization, governance, etc.) to ensure an executable program. Guidance for assessing programs for potential transition is provided in the Framework and Guidance for Assessing and Planning Program Transitions document on the CAE website.

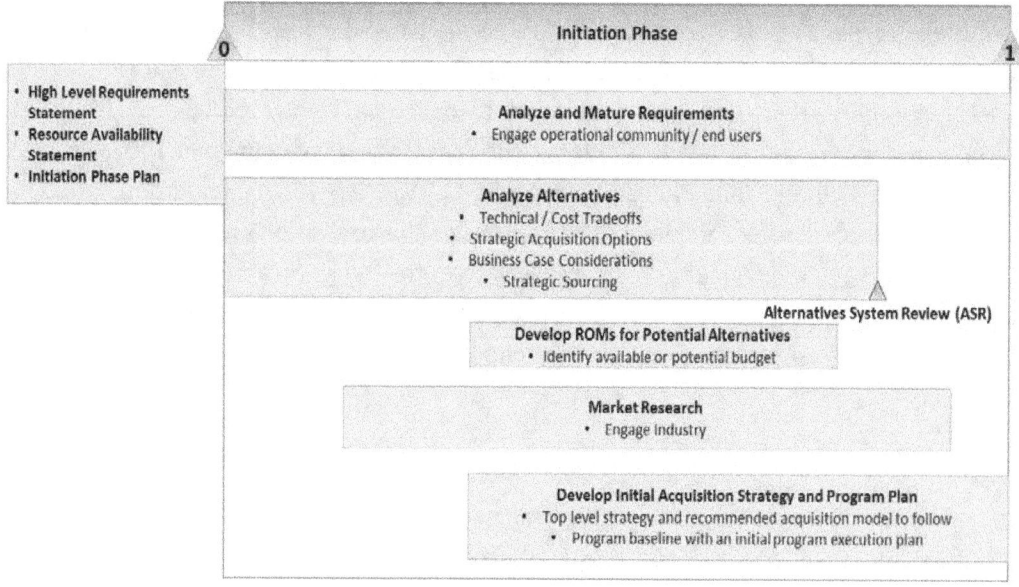

Figure 2. Initiation Phase Process View

VERSION 1.0

1   Decision Point 0

Decision Point 0 is a review that essentially kicks off the program, project, or related effort. The purpose of this review is to ensure that valid requirements and a team and budget are in place to conduct the initiation phase. The requirements requestor, herein referred to generically as the Requirements Owner (e.g., COMDEV, MATDEV), should be a validated forum or Operational Sponsor appropriately designated to speak for the specific community of interest. For enterprise services, requirements should be approved through the Services Portfolio Board. The requirements owner will identify a capability gap, and the set of requirements should be captured in a High-Level Requirements Statement. A Resource Availability Statement will accompany this document to validate that a budget and team is available to conduct the initiation phase activities, with roles and responsibilities of the team clearly outlined in the document. An Initiation Phase Plan is reviewed that describes at a high level the strategy to execute the initiation phase activities. The initiation phase may include pilot or prototype activities. These activities should be well defined with identified performance/success measures to support a program initiation decision. The Decision Authority will provide the team with guidance on the analysis, scope of effort, and strategy.

Key Questions:

The following questions must be addressed at Decision Point 0:

- Has the requirements owner identified and documented the operation need/capability gap and has the appropriate authority approved it?
- Have related capability gaps, analysis, or programs to include other services/agencies been explored to avoid duplication of efforts or leverage related work, funding, and resources?
- Has the requirement been examined for Doctrine, Organization, Training, Materiel, Leadership & Education, Personnel, and Facilitates (DOTMLPF) consideration?
- Is a team (or plan to assemble a team) in place to conduct the initiation phase activities?
- Is the initiation phase sufficiently funding?
- Have the team's authorities, expectations, and scope been clearly defined?

Information Required:

- High-Level Requirements Statement
- Resource Availability Statement
- Initiation Phase Plan

Decision Point 0 approval requires sufficient justification, initial analysis, and resources to conduct the initiation phase. The information required at Decision Point 0 is often done via limited resources as none has been formally committed at this stage of the acquisition. The Decision Authority may approve or reject a program to proceed to the initiation phase or may require additional analysis and resources before proceeding.

2   Analyze and Mature Requirements

During the initiation phase, the acquisition team will work closely with the requirements owner to mature the requirements. To set the stage for program requirements, the team should have a clear understanding of the Concept of Operations (CONOPS), operational objectives, and operational environment to set the stage for program requirements. The requirements owner should prioritize the operational requirements to plan development across releases, analyze alternatives, and support tradeoff analysis in the future. As requirements are matured, the team should collaborate frequently with the end users to ensure they effectively capture ongoing needs and development of a common understanding of current and future CONOPS. Collaboration with other stakeholders (e.g., operations, testers, enterprise architects, and contracting) is critical during the shaping of the requirements.

Programs with projected software development costs exceeding $15M are required to go through the Joint Capabilities Integration and Development System (JCIDS) process and encouraged to use the IT Box model, as described in the JCIDS Manual. The JROC approval of an Information System (IS) Initial Capabilities Document (ICD) at Decision Point 0 (or DP 1 at the latest binds the program and delegates future requirements oversight to a designated flag-level board at DISA or our customers. This approach enables more dynamic requirements management tailored documents and faster approvals at lower levels. For more information on the JCIDS IT Box concept, see the JCIDS Manual.

Requirements for enterprise services may be documented in a Service Level Description Document, describing the service to be delivered in terms of end-user experience, and validated by the Services Portfolio Board. Requirements for Acquisition of Services (AoS) are typically captured in a requirements document (e.g., Capability Needs Document (CND)) or tool and in the contract package work statement (e.g., Performance Work Statement (PWS)). All programs, projects, and services are required to have some level of documentation capturing a description of the capability to be delivered at the level of fidelity. This is to ensure a common understanding with the end users and to ensure that the program baseline (work activities, schedule, budget, etc.) is sufficient to deliver the expected capability.

The acquisition team will collaborate with the requirements owner on technical trends, commercial capabilities, technical standards, performance levels, and other acquisition factors. The alternatives analysis, market research, and strategy development conducted throughout the acquisition phase will be tightly integrated with the maturation of the program requirements.

The acquisition team will engage with the Operations Directorate, which will assign an operational integrator to the effort if appropriate. The operational integrator will assist the acquisition team in including Service Operations considerations into the requirements, to help ensure that the acquired capability can be efficiently and effectively operated using DISA's standardized Service Operations Framework.

> **Key Question:**
> - Have the requirements owner and end users documented and validated prioritized requirements?

3 Analyze Alternatives

A key activity of the initiation phase is to analyze the potential alternatives to acquire the product and/or service to satisfy the user's requirements. For most programs, this is *not* intended to be a comprehensive Analysis of Alternatives (AoA) at the level required for major defense acquisitions. The purpose is to ensure that appropriate alternatives, solutions, or courses of action have been considered prior to moving forward with an investment. This will be a tailored analysis that will appropriately leverage core elements of a formal AoA, business case, or cost benefit analysis. The tailoring will depend on the nature of the capability, program, and level of investment. The acquisition team will perform this analysis with active collaboration across DISA, DoD, other federal agencies, FFRDCs, contracting, and industry as appropriate.

An evaluation of alternatives should include not only performance/cost tradeoffs for technical solutions but also strategic acquisition options (service vs. product development effort), business model considerations (related service offerings and cost recovery), potential risks with each alternative, and strategic sourcing possibilities. The level of rigor required for this analysis will be scaled based on the size, scope, complexity, and interest of the acquisition effort (as with all DISA acquisition processes). For example, a small dollar-value sustainment project does not require extensive documentation, and the alternative analysis can be discussed at a summary level. On the other hand, a significant investment or major capability development may require a more formal AoA. MDAP and MAIS programs require AoA approval from OSD Cost Analysis and Program Execution (CAPE).

The foundation of this analysis is to identify the primary solution alternatives and then evaluate the cost and benefits associated with each one. Although meeting the capability and performance requirements is key, the solution must also be evaluated on program risk and total lifecycle cost. An understanding of the major cost drivers and the priority of requirements is necessary to identify cost/performance trade space, to explore alternative designs/systems/technologies, and to identify the optimal balance across these factors. This requires systems engineers to convey the technical design and details to the cost estimators to convey as thorough an understanding of the system as possible at this phase. As part of the cost estimate, the major cost drivers and cost estimates of potential alternatives should be discussed with the acquisition team.

The alternatives should incorporate solution, technical, and programmatic elements and need to be well defined to support the development of the estimated costs and benefits that form the basis for evaluation. Programs typically validate that the business case for the selected alternative on which a program is based is still sound at milestones or key decision points, especially if the program baseline or scope of requirements has changed significantly.

The solution alternatives often do not necessarily depend on a technology or system development. Solutions may be based on a change in operations, processes, or a new means of leveraging existing capabilities. These are important alternatives that are often overlooked due to the desire for new technology solutions. The initial identification of potential solutions should be broad to be sure all options are considered, but then the scope of the analysis should narrow to the most promising alternatives.

DISA's Chief Engineers Panel (CEP), as enterprise architects, must be involved at this early stage to help understand, guide, and integrate the solution into the DISA enterprise. With an enterprise view of the customers, technology, infrastructure, and resources, they can provide advice and guidelines on identifying and evaluating potential alternatives. The architects can help the team understand and interpret requirements and technology maturity, develop conceptual and logical models, align with related programs, and make connections across DISA's enterprise. As part of this analysis, the team should understand how each alternative would fit within the enterprise architecture and the associated benefits and risks.

The first step in the analysis is to define the capability required to meet the need and the associated technical or service-based solutions. DISA has close working relationships with various DoD organizations, including the intelligence community, research labs, the military departments, other defense agencies, and of course industry. Acquisition teams should leverage existing partnerships, where appropriate, to identify potential opportunities for solution alternatives. Technical solution alternatives should include a description of the system, product, or service intended to meet the capability and performance requirements with enough fidelity to support the initial program planning (cost estimate, schedule, and performance thresholds).

The next aspect of the analysis includes the various acquisition approaches that can be used to obtain the capability, including in conjunction with non-material DOTMLPF solutions. Many IT capabilities can be acquired in a variety of ways. For example, a capability could be developed using customized software, configured using COTS software and integrated into an existing system, or the capability can be entirely outsourced to a third party as a managed IT service. Each alternative has pros and cons, and the tradeoffs among DISA's acquisition capabilities, program risks, complexities, industry offerings, and other factors need to be considered.

Because a core aspect of DISA's mission is delivery of enterprise IT services to the defense community, this analysis should also consider DoD-level mission and business impacts (both financial and nonfinancial), risks, and sensitivities. The key is quantifying the benefits and costs to determine the optimal value; in many cases, the benefits are at the DoD level. The analysis should consider whether the acquisition should be an enterprise service (a capability that is acquired by DISA and designed for DoD-wide use), a service available within the enterprise (a capability that is acquired by DISA for a specific user but can also be made available to other DoD users), or a capability focused on a specific customer need. For more information, see the Business Case Analysis (BCA) page on ACQuipedia.

Refer to the Acquisition One Stop for examples of AoAs, Cost Benefit Analysis (CBA), and BCA formats and templates. For more information, see the Analysis of Alternatives section of the Defense Acquisition Guidebook and ACQuipedia.

Technical requirements should be based to the maximum extent practicable on open standards. Open Systems Architecture (OSA) is organized decomposition, using carefully defined execution boundaries, layered onto a framework of software and hardware shared services and a vibrant business model that facilitates competition. OSA is composed of five fundamental principles:

1. Modular designs based on standards, with loose coupling and high cohesion, that allow for independent acquisition of system components
2. Enterprise investment strategies, based on collaboration and trust, that maximize reuse of proven hardware system designs and ensure we spend the least to get the best
3. Transformation of the life cycle sustainment strategies for software intensive systems through proven technology insertion and software product upgrade techniques
4. Dramatically lower development risk through transparency of system designs, continuous design disclosure, and Government, academia, and industry peer reviews
5. Strategic use of data rights to ensure a level competitive playing field and access to alternative solutions and sources, across the life cycle.

The acquisition team should refer to the Office of the Deputy Assistant Secretary of Defense (ODASD) Systems Engineering site, as well as the Open System Architecture Contract Guidebook for Program Managers for tools, strategies, and processes.

As more and more IT capabilities become commoditized, the acquisition team should explore opportunities to leverage commercial service offerings and strategic sourcing opportunities. They should examine existing contract vehicles in DISA, across DoD, and the federal government (e.g., GSA) where the capabilities or elements of them (e.g., support) can be acquired. Alternatively, the acquisition team should evaluate if the services or commodities that need to be acquired should be available to the rest of DoD via a DISA-managed strategic sourcing contract. For more information about strategic sourcing, visit the Strategic Sourcing page on the AT&L/DPAP website.

The alternatives analysis should identify potential alternatives, provide sufficient analysis in the aspects discussed above, and capture the results in sufficient detail to give the decision maker enough information to determine the appropriate path forward to satisfy the requirement.

Acquisition team leaders may elect to conduct an Alternative Systems Review (ASR) at the end of an alternatives analysis. The ASR focuses technical efforts on requirements analysis to support a dialogue between the acquisition team and end users. They often lead to a draft performance specification for

the preferred materiel solution. The ASR should evaluate whether there is sufficient understanding of the technical maturity, feasibility, and risk of the preferred materiel solution, in terms of addressing the operational capability needs and meeting affordability, technology, and operational effectiveness and suitability goals.

A summary of this analysis will be presented to the Decision Authority to support Decision Point 1.

<u>**Key Questions:**</u>
Have alternatives been analyzed to consider:
- Technical maturity, risks, and integration?
- Strategies to acquire and manage the capabilities?
- Open systems architecture?
- Strategic sourcing opportunities?
- Price competitiveness with commercial offerings?

4   Develop ROMs for Potential Alternatives

As the team develops and analyzes alternatives they should develop rough order of magnitude (ROM) high-level cost estimates for each major alternative. Program affordability is of critical importance across the DoD, and DISA needs to have a solid understanding of the business case for each investment. The Decision Authority and acquisition team need to understand the costs, cost drivers, and funding strategy (to include cost recovery strategies for enterprise services). If the program proceeds after Decision Point 1, further refinement of cost estimates, systems engineering tradeoff analyses, affordability assessments, and competition assessments will be needed. Cost estimates should be either developed or validated by the Chief Financial Executive (CFE) support team. A Basis of Estimate template (currently not available at the time of publication) will help ensure that the full range of lifecycle costs, depicted in Figure 3 below, are included in the estimate.

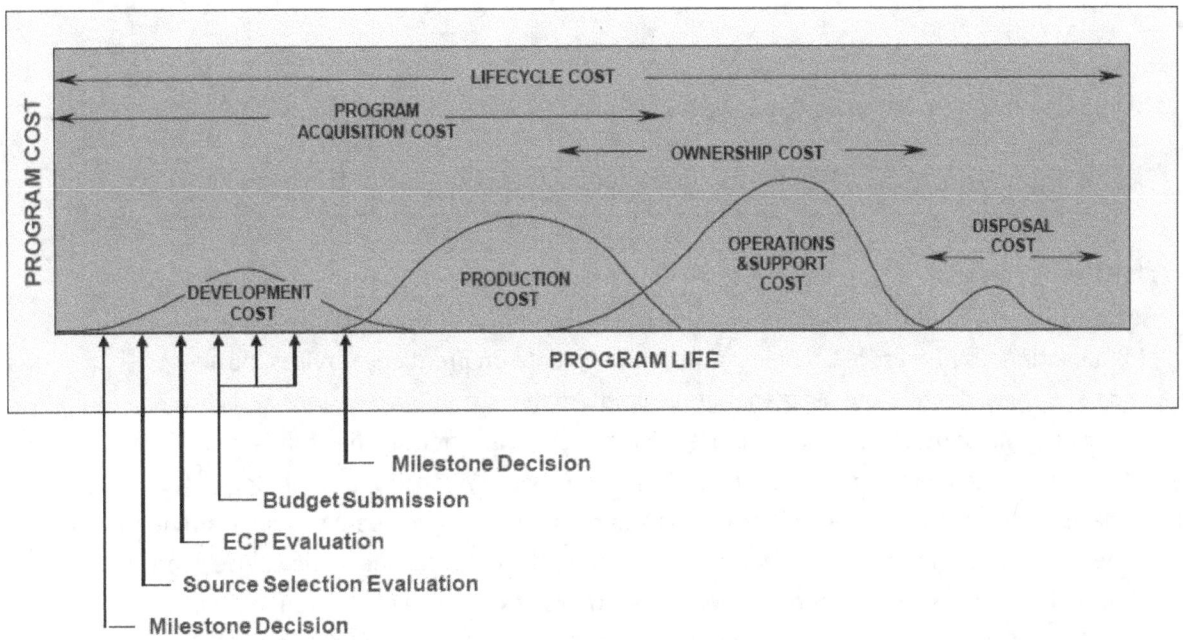

Figure 3 Program Lifecycle Costs Diagram

Cost estimates should leverage inputs from all the potential DISA Directorates and potential partner organizations that will conduct work activities in support of the program. It is essential to adequately consider post-deployment operational costs, as those costs are typically several times larger than pre-deployment acquisition costs. The operational integrator assigned by the Operations Directorate can assist in developing operational cost estimates.

Cost analysis that addresses cost risk (e.g., Monte Carlo simulation) and identifies the key elements that drive variability within the ROM cost estimate supports proactive management and decision making. To support DISA-wide analysis, the team should identify and capture the data that are or will be collected to validate business benefits and value. In addition to acquisition and ownerships costs, the ROMs developed to support the analysis of alternatives must include a quantification of the benefits associated with each alternative.

The acquisition team must also identify a strategy to fund the program. Appropriated funds are typically used for capability development and DWCF funds for delivery and sustainment of services. Direct reimbursable funding is appropriate for customer-specific services and/or support. The cost estimate should be captured as a multi-year funding profile, ideally total lifecycle costs, but at a minimum a FYDP funding profile. The funding profile should include the type of funding (RDT&E, Procurement, O&M, DWCF, etc.). If the recommended funding source is appropriated, the estimate should also include the recommended source of funding (e.g., Unfunded Requirements (UFRs), POM, and offsets) to help assess the funding risks. The cost estimates developed for the analysis will become the basis for establishing the program cost/budget baseline for program initiation.

> **Key Questions:**
> - Were ROMs developed for the major alternatives?
> - What was the basis for estimates?
> - Have major cost drivers been identified for affordability tradeoffs?

5 Market Research

Market research and active industry engagement are critical elements for shaping the early acquisition strategy. It is a continuous process of collecting and analyzing data on products, services, business practices, and vendor capabilities and using that information to make suitable decisions and choices about the acquisition of goods and services and the pricing of services offered. The team should conduct and leverage ongoing research across DISA, Defense Services/Agencies, other federal agencies, and commercial industry to examine related programs and technologies. The team should examine the companies, the technologies used, the strategies implemented, the results, issues, price performance, and any best practices and lessons learned. In most cases, there are ongoing efforts to maintain current knowledge of the technology and market in areas of DISA core competence that can be leveraged by updating or focusing the scope of previous research. Tools for market research include Requests for Information (RFIs), industry days/pre-solicitation conferences, vendor one-on-ones, querying government/commercial databases, Internet research, etc. Market research, as in the case of *all* acquisition processes, should be scaled based on the size, scope, complexity, and interest of the effort.

For more information on market research, visit the Small Business Administration's (SBA) site on recommended practices (information is not limited to small business acquisitions). Additionally, the Office of Management and Budget (OMB) Memorandum on "'Mythbusting' – Addressing Misconceptions to Improve Communication with Industry during the Acquisition Process" provides additional tips and strategies on communicating with industry.

> **Key Questions:**
> - Does market research support the choice of solution alternatives, analysis, and strategies?
> - Did the team leverage appropriate market research tools and opportunities?

6 Develop Initial Acquisition Strategy and Program Plan

The maturity of the requirements, alternatives analysis, and market research should all help to shape the program's initial acquisition strategy. In this early initiation phase, the acquisition strategy should contain sufficient information to convey an understanding of how the required capabilities will be acquired. It should be based on an acquisition model that is the best fit for the recommended solution and strategy from the alternatives analysis and market research. The initial acquisition strategy should include a categorization of program type, identification of products and services to be acquired

correlated to the contracting strategy, and recommended program baseline of cost, schedule, and performance.

Risk management is a fundamental aspect of good program management. Acquisition teams and key stakeholders should conduct a structured risk identification and management session. Capturing, discussing, prioritizing, mitigating, and managing risks will be integral to the development of the acquisition strategy. A risk management process should be developed with individuals assigned to regularly identify, assess, manage, and report on risks and mitigation strategies. For additional information on Risk Management, see the Risk Management Guide for DoD Acquisition.

The initial high-level program plan is based on the work conducted for the analysis of alternatives using the cost, schedule, and performance parameters for the recommended solution. The schedule should include all the milestones or key decision points, as well as operational and engineering reviews at appropriate points in the acquisition (e.g., NRRB and CEP). Enough fidelity of the program plan is required to support a program initiation decision. Typically this requires a high-level description of the solution, engineering approach, architecture context, contracting strategy, etc. The program plan should also include roles and responsibilities and identify the Decision Authority for the acquisition.

It is important to keep the program strategy and plan at the right level to support the decision for program initiation without investing too many resources in planning details of an effort that may not move forward. The initial program plan will form the program baseline if a positive program initiation decision supporting the recommended alternative is made.

As the program progresses through the acquisition lifecycle, there should be clear criteria or expectations to ensure that the program is meeting its intended value. Though each decision point offers a checkpoint for approval to the next acquisition phase, DISA must remain cognizant of underperforming or lower priority efforts. If changes to the operational environment, requirements, technology, costs, budgets, technical performance, contractors, or other factors result in a severe degrading of the program's value, these need to be understood and reviewed by appropriate stakeholders.

For more information on Acquisition Strategies and Program Plans, reference Chapter IV, Section 3.

Note: We're examining the structure/alignment/integration of acquisition strategy and program plan.

Key Questions:
- Does the initial Acquisition Strategy acquire the capabilities effectively and efficiently?
- Does the analysis support the Acquisition Strategy well?
- Does the proposed program baseline provide enough fidelity to support a program initiation decision?

7 Decision Point 1

The purpose of this decision point is to make the decision on whether to establish and invest in a program to deliver the proposed solution. This depends on whether the solution alternative is well justified, the proposed plan is viable, the benefits are worth the cost, there is reasonable expectation of meeting the requirements, funding and billets are available, and the work aligns with DISA strategic objectives. At Decision Point 1 the Decision Authority (DA) reviews the initial analysis, costs, and strategy. Depending on the level, resources required, and type of program or service, the DA may provide approval to proceed to an Acquisition Review Board (ARB) and establish the program baseline for execution. An NRRB and/or CEP may be required to support an ARB decision, depending on the level, phase, and type of program. If there is a significant investment required, potential operational impact, program/integration dependencies, long-term sustainment costs, and/or other high risks, the decision may require additional forums such as the Health Assessment Review Tool (HART) or Executive Committee (EXCOM).

The DA at Decision Point 1 will determine if a pre-Milestone B or pre-Decision Point 2 (depending on the acquisition model) is required. If required, the acquisition team will need to obtain DA review and approval prior to the release of the Request for Proposal (RFP). If it is not required, the acquisition team will only need to seek DA review and approval prior to contract award at Milestone B or Decision Point 2.

In some cases, existing capabilities or programs are transitioned to DISA from external sources and are re-baselined as a DISA program or enterprise service offering. Projects of this nature should conduct a program transition assessment to support a transition decision. This will also facilitate transition planning and help to establish an appropriate program baseline. Guidance for assessing programs for potential transition is provided in the Framework and Guidance for Assessing and Planning Program Transitions document on the CAE website.

At Decision Point 1, acquisition team leaders should be prepared to answer each of the key questions highlighted in the blue boxes above. Additionally, the following information is required for Decision Point 1 approval.

Information Required:
The following documents are required for Decision Point 1 approval:
- Documented Requirements
- Alternative Analysis
- Cost estimate (multiyear funding profile and total lifecycle cost)
- Market research
- Acquisition Strategy
- Initial Program Plan/Baseline

8   Special Consideration for Pilots

A pilot is the first or initial phase or issuance of a model, system, or item used as a control to test a proposal. Pilots can be used for technology evaluation, operational concept, requirements validation, user interest/acceptance (e.g., market testing), limited fielding, or product/solution testing or validation.

The evaluation criteria to determine what is considered successful at the end of the pilot need to be consistent with the stated purpose of the pilot. Therefore, at the initiation of a pilot, the acquisition team will produce a Pilot Charter. The Pilot Charter should identify the capability being piloted, a schedule and level of effort, a high-level ROM, and a pilot execution strategy. The Decision Authority will provide a budget for the pilot and establish evaluation criteria to define completion and success of that pilot. When the pilot has been completed, the Decision Authority will evaluate the pilot's success against the pre-established evaluation criteria to determine a way ahead. Options may include authorizing a new pilot effort, incorporating the pilot into an existing acquisition program/project, or designating the pilot as an independent program/project that will reenter the acquisition process at a specific Decision Point.

For acquisitions of capabilities which involve operations, pilots also provides an opportunity to iteratively refine the operational concept and reduce operational risk. The operational integrator assigned to the project by the DISA Operations directorate can assist in identifying the operational artifacts and reviews which will be required prior to executing the pilot, and the operational integration outcomes that can be pursued during the pilot.

Chapter III DISA IT Acquisition Models

Following the initiation phase, the program/project will continue with a defined IT acquisition model. Each of the models defined in this section has been proactively tailored based on the acquisition steps required for the specific type of acquisition. Table 2 provides guidance on which of the DISA acquisition models can be used based on the IT product or service that is being acquired. ***Within a model, the acquisition team leader shall further tailor based on the type, size, complexity, risk, and interest of what is being acquired.*** The first responsibility of the acquisition team leader is to use practical judgment when scaling the processes and documentation for each acquisition. As part of the analysis i n the initiation phase, the acquisition team should recommend a model to follow for Decision Point 1.

Table 2 provides top-level guidance of which model to use based on what is being acquired. As IT is evolving to more of a service delivery model, there are often multiple approaches to acquire a capability. Each model comes with pros and cons that should be considered when deciding on a model. The analysis and research completed in the initiation phase should provide some clear options to consider. When deciding on the right acquisition model to use, the acquisition team should consider:

1. Are there existing COTS/GOTS products that could be leveraged for most requirements?
2. Are there vendors that can deliver the capability as a service?
3. What are the schedule drivers from an operational, programmatic, and technical perspective? This can range for an urgent operational need to the expected lifespan of the technology or program.
4. Are there budgetary constraints—amount, appropriation type, and source?
5. What is the level of technical performance required and the amount of change in scope and requirements?
6. Will this be delivered as an enterprise service? What are the pricing strategies/factors to consider?
7. Is there a considerable difference in cost estimates for various alternatives (development, COTS, Service)? This includes total ownership costs of development, integration, delivery, operations, sustainment, and evolution.
8. What are the primary operational, technical, and programmatic risks?
9. Do Information Assurance or security classifications drive or prohibit a particular approach?
10. What is the level of technical maturity and system complexity?
11. What level does the acquisition need to be integrated with the enterprise architecture, platforms, and related systems
12. The amount and level of government expertise to manage program—this includes systems engineering and contracting, among other acquisition specialties.
13. Can DISA integrate competitive pressures on the contractors throughout the program's lifecycle to keep performance high and costs low? Could segmenting the work across multiple contractors/models provide benefits that outweigh the risks?

DISA IT Acquisition Guidebook

14. Can some elements (e.g., documentation, help desk, training) be bundled with other programs/projects/services?

Table 2. DISA Acquisition Models Based on What You're Acquiring

	IT Products and Services *"What You're Acquiring"*	DISA Acquisition Models *"How You're Acquiring IT"*
Development	DoD unique software delivered via multiple short releases	**1. Agile Development**
	Small DoD unique application (includes mobile apps)	
	Minor enhancements or maintenance to an existing program	
	Major enhancement to an existing program	
	DoD unique hardware and software delivered via multi-year increments	**2. Incremental Development**
COTS/GOTS	Customizing COTS software for DoD business processes (non-mission requirements)	**3. Defense Business Systems**
	Establishing broad use contract vehicle for Non-Developmental Item (NDI) COTS/GOTS products and enterprise licensing agreements	**4. IT Commodities**
	COTS/GOTS products and services to be integrated into an existing DoD unique software or system	**5. Integrated COTS/GOTS**
	COTS/GOTS products and services to deliver an IT Environment – IaaS and PaaS	
	Configuring a suite of COTS/GOTS products to adapt and deliver as an enterprise service	**6. Enterprise Services**
	Integrating COTS/GOTS products to adapt and deliver as an enterprise service	
	Customization of COTS/GOTS products to adapt and deliver as an enterprise service	
	IT portfolios and programs that satisfy a long term capability requirement on a continuous basis.	**7. Continuous Capability Delivery**
Services	IT capabilities developed, integrated, and maintained via a Services contract	**8. Managed IT Services**
	Manpower support for help desk, network management and operations, leased data circuits and transport services, and other professional support services	**9. IT Support Services**

23

DISA IT Acquisition Guidebook

1 Agile Development (Model 1)

The agile development model is used for the development and/or customization of DoD unique software applications or services that require continual capability enhancements over time to stay current with dynamic warfighter requirements. As illustrated in Figure 4, the delivery is via small, frequent releases, generally hosted within an environment that enables efficient transition across development, test, and operational environments. The cycle times for capability delivery (releases, sprints, etc.,) will depend on the complexity, interdependency, and potential impact to users of enhancements.

Some of the key characteristics of this acquisition model include:

- A dynamic process to regularly update, refine, and reprioritize requirements
- Active user engagement throughout the design, development, and testing process to provide insight on operations and feedback on demonstrated capabilities
- Contract strategy and timelines that support frequent capability releases
- Releases and /or sprints for managed delivery of capability enhancements responsive to changes in operations, technology, and budgets
- Integrated testing, certification often automated across the lifecycle to support short timelines
- Development environment that supports rapid transition to production/operations
- Designed-to enterprise architectures, standards, and interfaces

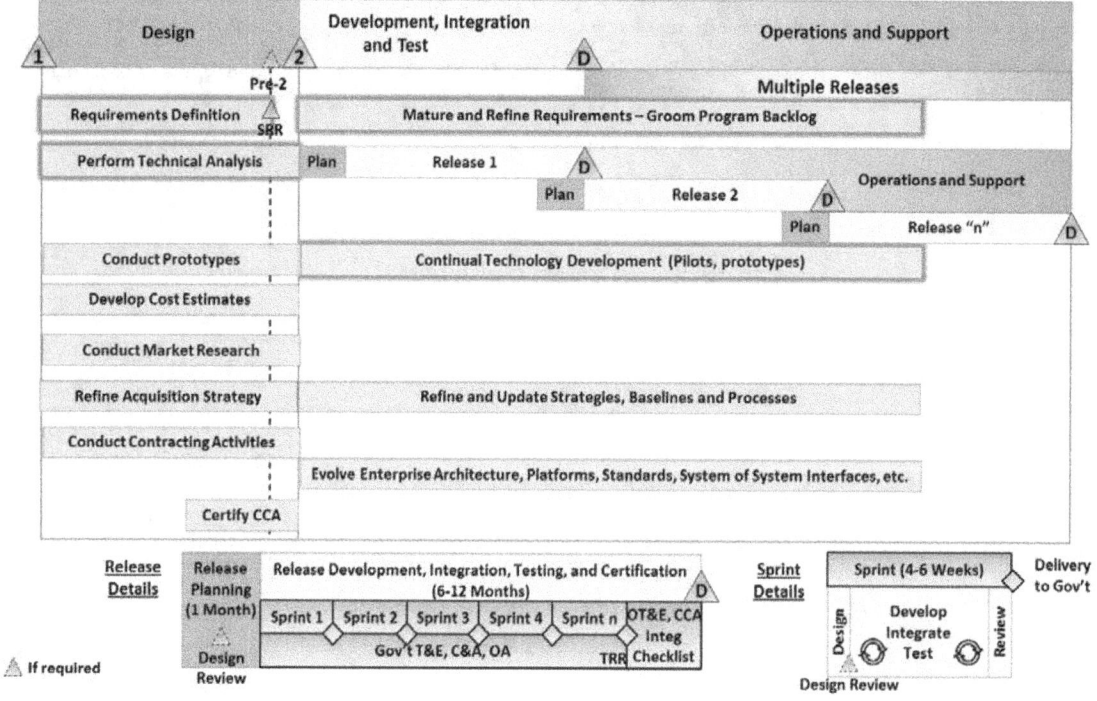

Figure 4. Agile Development Model Process View

1.1 Design Phase

The objectives of the design phase are to develop a robust design and technical baseline that will provide the initial capability delivery and enable rapid insertion of future capabilities. The intended outcome is an optimized design with some demonstrated ability to satisfy the requirements and provide an affordable solution for sustainment. The design should maximize the use of open architecture, standards, common development environments, etc. such as an Ozone widget or storefront framework. The design should also maximize the use of related infrastructure such as portals, capacity services, milCloud, etc. and ensure alignment with JIE objectives. The design should ensure that the capability will be integrated with DISA's operational monitoring/management processes and tools, so that it can be efficiently and effectively operated. The design will leverage, align, and evolve with enterprise architectures, standards, and interfaces. Requirements will be matured, reprioritized, and evolve based on the design and initial analysis.

Activities to be performed in this phase continue building on the documents and decisions from the initiation phase. In addition to the design of the solution, this phase starts with developing another level of detail of the program implementation plan to enable effective program execution. At this point, the acquisition team leader should have an effective integrated management framework in place to include an Integrated Master Schedule, program controls, Work Breakdown Structure, multiyear spend plan, performance measures, etc. The following Design Phase activities, documents, and plans are typical for this phase.

1.1.1 Manage Requirements

Agile development methods require a dynamic but well-managed requirements process. The requirements that form the basis for the program need to be documented to identify the set of capabilities and related performance parameters to be delivered.

The agile requirements process needs a governance strategy and/or forum to centralize the user feedback, validation, and prioritization of existing and new requirements as each spiral is defined. Requirements allocated for each release or sprint should be documented for traceability and for tracking completion of the total set of program requirements. Requirements management tools help simplify the documentation and traceability, especially when there is a rapid cycle time for releases and sprints. Rather than locking in requirements for a large system in a lengthy document, requirements can be captured in a database or related tool to be further refined, allocated, decomposed, reprioritized, and added/deleted over time. The database should ideally have a configuration management feature to allow the stakeholders to keep track of changes over time. In an agile development method, there should be an initial plan for allocation of requirements for each spiral, to be refined as requirements are updated, design matures, and feedback from initial releases is available. Requirements for sprints, within releases, are often allocated just prior to or as part of the design for that release.

Requirements are often defined, analyzed, translated, and refined using various approaches such as user stories, operational architecture views, scenarios, display mock-ups, CONOPS (early phase focused on requirements vs. later CONOPS focused on how system will be operated), or use cases to convey the true operational need clearly with supporting acceptance criteria. These tools often follow a standardized format. Agile programs manage the total set of requirements as a backlog of requirements. Feedback from previous releases, inputs from the warfighters, budget and resource constraints, and other factors will influence the requirements backlogs.

Strong partnerships and continuous collaboration with the requirements community are critical to ensure that requirements are technically achievable and affordable to support cost/performance decisions. Requirements documents should provide information about the relative priorities of requirements to support cost/performance tradeoffs.

For additional information on managing requirements, reference Chapter IV, Section 1.

> **Best Practice Example**
>
> Global Combat Support System-Joint (GCSS-J) is an ACAT-IA DISA program that started using agile in 2008 for Block 7. Each Block is decomposed into a series of Increments, and the Increments are divided into Sprints. GCSS-J employs a continuous release planning process that is based on a time-boxed schedule. Each Sprint begins with and operates on a monthly iteration cycle that includes a 5-day planning period, 20-day code development, and 7-day limited user assessment. Four iterations are bundled into a release that is delivered to the field every 6 months. The program also holds weekly Systems Engineering Meetings and twice-weekly Functional Requirements Working Group meetings with the J4 sponsor to groom the requirements backlog and plan for future releases.

Key Questions:
- Does the program have a dynamic process to regularly update, refine, and reprioritize requirements?
- Does each release and sprint have a defined schedule?
- Does each requirement/user story planned for the release/sprint have an associated cost and acceptance/performance criteria?
- Are users actively engaged throughout the design, development, and testing process to provide feedback for each spiral?
- Is integration with Service Operations processes and tools iteratively refined and evaluated as part of each spiral?

1.1.2 Perform Technical Analysis

1.1.2.1 Develop a Technical Baseline

The technical baseline manages and tracks the evolution of requirements, designs, configurations, development, integration, test, and other elements. It should serve as the foundation for the other programmatic elements (acquisition strategy, cost, test, etc.). As the program progresses through the

acquisition lifecycle, the technical baseline will mature with increasing rigor, number of data sources, and fidelity of details.

In an agile environment, the funding profile and baseline will likely include a level of funding allocated for enhancements with sufficient margin to provide program flexibility. Each requirement should have a cost associated with it and a relative priority. The scope of each release will likely be time boxed and address the highest priority requirements based on available budget. The program baseline and budget should be structured to allow this agility because the scope of each release is too dynamic to effectively budget and baseline.

During this phase, the acquisition team should focus on the software development environment to enable agile development. This includes the use of DISA's Rapid Access Computing Environment (RACE) and milCloud, along with any commercial products (often determined by the developer(s)). These tools enable effective requirements management and rapid transition from development, to test, and to production environments. The designs should maximize the use of open and modular architectures and applications like Ozone widget frameworks or storefronts.

For additional information on developing a technical baseline, reference Chapter IV, Section 2.1.

> **Key Questions:**
> - Is the program leveraging existing hardware platforms and enterprise architectures, standards, and interfaces?
> - Does the design integrate mature technologies and align to DISA architectures, standards, and interfaces?
> - Does the design anticipate technological evolution?
> - Does the design consider Mission Assurance?

In developing and maturing the design of the program, it is critical to have an understanding of each element and requirement and its impact on cost, schedule, technical performance, and risk. In an agile environment, the key is to get to the development phase quickly after doing some due diligence in the planning stages. This tradeoff analysis shouldn't be a lengthy drawn-out process serving as a pre-requisite to development. The team should get the framework and foundational elements in place during the design phase and establish an *iterative process* to assess tradeoffs throughout development.

For additional information on conducting systems engineering tradeoff analysis, reference Chapter IV, Section 2.2.

> **Key Question:**
> - Has a sufficient systems engineering/cost tradeoff analysis been conducted?

1.1.3 Conduct Prototypes

Prototypes can be used to reduce development, integration, and other risks commensurate with the cost and schedule considerations of the program. They can be done at the system, subsystem, or component level or simply focus on technology maturity. Given that the design phase is intended to be succinct, prototypes should focus on influencing the design and should continue throughout development to support future releases. Pilots are the first issuance of a model, system, or item used as a control to test a proposal. Prototypes and pilots can be leveraged or integrated with a technology demonstration external to DISA. They can be designed for developmental purposes only or released to a limited operational environment for operational assessment and user feedback. Integration into DISA's Service Operations Framework should be considered as part of prototype iterations, as delaying this integration may increase technical risk and cost.

For additional information on conducting prototypes and pilots, reference Chapter IV, Section 9.

1.1.4 Develop Cost Estimate

Each program or project must develop and maintain a lifecycle cost estimate. Cost estimating in an agile environment is an emerging discipline. Because agile development typically involves time-boxed releases (e.g., six months), the cost driver for software centric projects is often the labor costs for the developers, testers, and related agile team members. Estimating the costs of all the requirements in the program backlog is often a challenge. The fidelity of the estimates increases once you have a development team on board to help estimate the level of work for each requirement/user story, and it further improves with subsequent releases.

Within an agile development project, each requirement is converted into a user story with acceptance criteria. Using any number of potential scales, the development team assigns a number (e.g., story point) for each user story. A small, simple story could be a one point, whereas a moderate story could be an eight point, which means it will take eight times as long to develop. Some teams estimate in hours. As development progresses, they track many metrics, including velocity—how many points can the team accomplish in a sprint and release. They then adjust the scope of the subsequent sprint/release based on their velocity and the estimated points for each story in the backlog.

The team will regularly reassess the points of the backlog items based on insight from recent releases. This iterative approach increases the fidelity of estimates over time. This is a very different approach from traditional cost estimating practices with complex cost models tied to software lines of code or elements of a Work Breakdown Structure (WBS).

In addition to the development cost described above, cost estimates should include the entire life of a program including operations and sustainment and disposal. "Should cost" and "will cost" targets will be established and used to support contract negotiations, and profit incentive structures, as well as being used as a management tool.

For additional information on cost estimates for Agile development, visit Estimating on Agile Projects by Scott Ambler and Agile Estimating and Planning by Mike Cohn. For more information on cost estimates and "should cost" management, reference Chapter IV Section 4, DAG Chapter 3.7 Principles for Lifecycle Cost Estimates, and the Better Buying Power website.

1.1.5 Conduct Market Research

Active engagement with industry is critical to program success. If the program is leveraging an existing contract vehicle, the acquisition team should closely collaborate with the contractors on the contract vehicle. In addition to broad industry collaboration to understand technologies or solicit ideas, DISA will need to have an ongoing partnership with industry to discuss upcoming trends, new technology, and DISA's future needs.

Small, frequent, and iterative releases under an agile acquisition provide an opportunity to increase small business participation. The acquisition team should consider the use of a small business set-aside contract vehicle to find small businesses that specialize in agile development and facilitation. The acquisition team should consider pursuing industry engagement strategies that target small businesses, for example, advisory multistep strategies, small business RFIs, and working with the DISA Office of Small Business Programs.

For additional information on conducting market research, reference Chapter IV, Section 6.2.

1.1.6 Refine Acquisition Strategy

Leveraging the analysis completed in the initiation and design phases, the acquisition team must develop a comprehensive acquisition strategy commensurate with the program's size, risk, and complexity.

For additional information on acquisition strategy, reference Chapter IV, Section 3.

Key Questions:
- Is the program/service a candidate for a DISA standard processing environment (e.g., RACE, FORGE.mil)?
- Are the resources requirements for the DISA standard processing environment and the associated migration activities adequately addressed in the acquisition strategy?
- If the product/service is not a candidate for the standard processing environment, has a waiver been obtained?
- Does the strategy plan specify the use of DISA standardized Service Operations tools (e.g. for pro-active monitoring, service-level compliance, and trouble-ticketing)?
- Does the strategy plan specify the operations functions that will support the capability (e.g. cognizant Service Desk, Technical Management, IT Operations Management, and Access Management teams) and how they will be resourced?

The acquisition team should finalize the Systems Engineering Plan, Test and Evaluation Strategy (Test and Evaluation Management Plan (TEMP) for formal ACAT programs), Lifecycle Sustainment Plan (LCSP), and Acquisition Program Baseline (APB). For additional information on each of these acquisition documents, reference Chapter IV, Section 3.

Given the dynamic nature of agile programs, careful consideration must be given to the scope of the APB. An APB is not required for each release (e.g., six month), but it could cover a timeframe of five years or more spanning multiple releases.

Key Questions:
- Is testing and certification integrated and automated throughout the lifecycle to support short timelines?
- Does the program have sufficient SE processes, reviews?
- Is there a change management process for design and requirements changes?

1.1.7 Contracting Activities

The program should engage with the DISA Procurement and Logistics Directorate as early as possible. It is important for the acquisition to keep the Contracting Officer well informed of the acquisition strategy and requirements changes so that the contracting strategy can be designed to fit the needs of the program. This is especially important when using an agile development process to ensure that the contracting process does not become an obstacle to

> **Best Practice Recommendation**
>
> Engage users and testers in developing the contract scope, evaluation criteria, incentives, and terms and conditions to ensure the contracting activity fully supports all needs and considerations.

program delivery. Agile contracting processes need to be deliberate and well executed without impeding program delivery. To foster a culture that adopts agile development, current contracting strategies need to be reevaluated to provide a flexible business environment for IT programs. Some of the fundamental needs of agile IT contracting are:

- Streamlined contracting processes that enable capability delivery every 6–12 months
- Flexible contract scope with the ability to refine requirements through the development process
- Qualified vendors that have knowledge and experience with nontraditional development practices
- Close working relationship between the PMO and Contracting Office

Contracting in an agile environment requires innovative approaches and a change in business culture to achieve the speed and flexibility required to support agile. There is no singular recommended contracting path or strategy for an agile implementation. However, establishing an agile environment with flexible contract options and streamlined processes are universally key components of agile

contracting. The selection of a contracting strategy should be based on several factors and considerations, one of which is the risk tolerance of the organization, current contracting environment and processes, and the amount of dedicated contracting support available for the acquisition. To implement a contract that supports an agile approach, the program can consider using any of these contracting options:

- **Multiple Award Contract (MAC) Vehicle.** Award an IDIQ contract to multiple qualified Agile developers. Contractors compete for individual task orders for each agile release or a bundled set of releases. A MAC IDIQ contract allows the program to maintain continuous competition; however, the time required to compete individual task orders can inhibit agile development timelines. Ideally, the ordering process for individual task orders should be streamlined to ~4–6 weeks to keep pace with agile timelines. Frequent, small developments provide valuable contractor performance data and feedback to shape future orders. Additionally, multiple small releases can enable greater small business participation.

- **Single Award IDIQ Contract Vehicle.** Award an IDIQ contract to a single awardee. Each agile release or a bundled set of releases can be issued on a task order. Because individual task orders do not have to be competed, this strategy is more streamlined than a MAC IDIQ strategy; however, it loses the benefits that can be gained from a continuous competition environment. This strategy should be used if the cost of administering multiple contracts exceeds the expected benefits; work is integrally related— only a single company can reasonably perform; market research shows favorable pricing, terms, and conditions can be achieved if a single award is made; and the ceiling is <$103M (including options) unless MDA justifies in writing.

- **GSA Blanket Purchase Agreement (BPA).** The program can issue a competitive BPA off an existing GSA Schedule contract (e.g., Schedule 70). Each agile sprint, release, or bundled set of releases can be issued as a call order once the

> **Best Practice Example**
>
> PEO-MA is using an innovative strategy to streamline the contracting process for agile development. PEO-MA competed and awarded a Blanket Purchase Agreement (BPA) under GSA IT Schedule 70. PEO-MA awarded BPAs to three small business contractors, using a Best Value trade-off process, to provide engineering support services for agile development efforts. Each agile sprint is competed at the BPA-level using Lowest Priced Technically Acceptable (LPTA) evaluation strategy. The overall BPA strategy has streamlined the contracting process for quick-turnaround BPA call orders for short-term agile engineering support requirements.

BPA is in place. The BPA can be issued to a single vendor or a pool of qualified vendors, to include small business set-asides. The key difference between a GSA BPA and agency-issued IDIQ contract is the required use of GSA-established contract labor categories and terms and conditions. Also, GSA call orders are limited to fixed-price or time-and-material contract types.

31

- **Increment Based Contract.** The program competes and issues a single contract to a single Agile developer. The program then incrementally funds the contract for each agile release, or a set of releases, that has been predefined on the contract using option periods and optional tasks. The benefit with this strategy is that a separate task order does not need to be issued for each phase, increment, or release, thus decreasing the amount of time to contract for each agile release. The PWS needs to be structured in such a way that each release or set of releases, with associated deliverables, are clearly delineated as individual contract/task order line item numbers (CLINs) and/or option periods. The drawback to this contract is that the program needs to have some understanding of the requirements up front, or the work involved with each release, so that contractors can develop a proposal and pricing against each CLIN and option period.

- **Single Award Contract.** This is the traditional contract award model where the program competes and issues a single contract to an Agile developer. This strategy is often difficult to implement because it does not easily allow for the adjustment of the scope of work, contract pricing, and level of effort between each release. However, once the contract is in place, there is little the program has to do between each release. This contract strategy offers the least flexibility to make adjustments to the contract based on information and experience gained from previous releases, and in most cases, it is used to temporarily staff an agile development effort.

Agile IT contracting strategies need to prevent contracting timelines from delaying delivery timelines. Just as the agile IT approach reflects the rapid pace of IT advances, agile IT development cycles demand the use of rapid contracting processes to ensure that contracting activities meet development timelines. Today IT contract awards solicited via full and open competition can take 12–18 months to execute. This timeline impacts agile delivery if not built into the initial program planning.

Large-scale development contracts can be decomposed into multiple, small contract actions, some of which can be accomplished in parallel. This requires a disciplined process to manage the solicitation, award, and execution of multiple contract actions, as well as a streamlined ordering process to expedite contract award.

Many processes exist for managing multiple, small, related contracting efforts. The applicable agile IT guidelines include:

- Engage users and testers in developing the contract scope, evaluation criteria, incentives, and terms and conditions to ensure the contracting activity fully supports all needs and considerations.
- Develop templates and standard business processes to streamline ordering procedures and ensure the quick execution of Task/Delivery Orders—in weeks rather than months. Task Orders that take months to execute will delay development cycles.

32

- Work with the contracting office to develop standard Statement of Work (SOW) language and implement the use of contract templates to standardize terms and conditions and business processes. This helps to expedite contracting activities and reduce costs.
- Understand the dedicated contracting process and associated timelines for executing Task/Delivery Orders. Program managers should become familiar with contracting documentation and approval requirements and form a partnership with the contracting office to enable an agile business environment.

For additional more information on contracting, reference Chapter IV, Section 6.

Key Question:
- Do the contract strategy and timelines support frequent capability releases?

1.1.8 Certify Clinger-Cohen Act

Clinger-Cohen Act (CCA) compliance by DISA CIO is required. For additional information on CCA compliance and certification, reference Chapter IV, Section 8.

1.2 Decision Point 2

At Decision Point 2, the Decision Authority reviews analyses and strategies for approval to develop the capabilities, ensures that the design integrates mature technologies that is aligned to enterprise architectures, and validates program affordability to meet validated requirements within the available budget. The Decision Authority approves the release of the RFP or contract award.

In addition to the key questions identified above, the acquisition team should be prepared to answer the following standard questions at Decision Point 2:

Standard Questions for Decision Point 2:
- Are the program requirements validated and prioritized?
- Have rigorous cost estimates been conducted?
- Is the program affordable within the available budget?
- Does the contract strategy address risk, incentives, data rights, and competition across the lifecycle?
- Does the team actively engage industry to shape strategy?
- Is testing integrated and scaled based on program risk?
- Is there a transition plan to deploy capabilities?
- Is there a plan to operate the capability in accordance with the DISA Service Operations Framework?
- Is there a realistic Integrated Master Schedule?
- Has the program identified and mitigated risks?
- Does the strategy satisfy the customer's requirements?
- Is the strategy designed to maximize competition?

- How will the contract type minimize risk to the government?
- Are existing contract vehicles available for the required services? If not, should DISA develop an enterprise contract vehicle for this service?
- Does the strategy appropriately leverage contract type and objective incentives to motivate contractors to exceed minimum performance requirements?
- Have conflict-of-interest issues been addressed and eliminated or mitigation plans established?

The following information is also required for Decision Point 2 approval:

Information Required at Decision Point 2:
- Acquisition Strategy (includes Technical Analysis, Market Research, Pilot/Prototype Results, Information Support Plan, Technical Data Rights Strategy, Systems Engineering Plan, Architecture Views, Test and Evaluation Management Plan, and Lifecycle Sustainment Plan)
- Capability Requirements Document
- Concept of Operations
- Services Operations Annex
- Acquisition Program Baseline
- Cost Estimate
- Acquisition Plan
- Request for Proposal and Other Contracting Docs (e.g., PWS, QASP, SSP)
- Service Level Agreements (when applicable)
- Business Processes Reengineering (when applicable)
- Clinger-Cohen Act Compliance

The acquisition team will prepare an Acquisition Decision Memorandum (ADM) and the Decision Authority will sign it. The ADM will capture the key decisions in the meeting, any action items for the acquisition team, and any guidance or deviations from policy and guidance for criteria for the next acquisition phase and deployment decision.

1.3 Development, Integration, and Test Phase

The objectives of the development, integration, and test phase are to complete the acquisition of the COTS/GOTS products, complete integration/configuration and adapt the product to operate within the DISA enterprise, and offer the product or service in the DISA Service Catalog (if applicable).

Activities to be performed in this phase include performing the customization and configuration of the COTS/GOTS products, testing and obtaining the necessary certifications and documents to add to the DISA enterprise, and offering the adapted product to customers.

1.3.1 Mature and Refine Requirements—Groom Program Backlog

The acquisition team should continue to mature and refine requirements activities conducted in the design phase. Requirements in an Agile development are managed via backlogs versus formal requirements documents. Backlogs are an evolving prioritized queue, or they are requirements from the operational and technical stakeholders that are managed in databases and related tools. To continually prioritize and evolve requirements, a Product Owner, working with the user community and other stakeholders, actively grooms the backlogs. Figure 5 provides an overview of an Agile requirements process.

When the team is planning for a new release, the highest priority requirements that can be completed within the established release schedule are pulled from a program backlog. A release backlog is created from the program backlog to regularly prioritize and manage the release requirements. From the release backlog, a sprint is created for the highest priority requirements that can be completed within the established sprint schedule (~6 weeks). The scope of the sprint is locked once the development team commits to the scope of work. The release scope, on the other hand, is more dynamic. Sprint demos may identify new features or defects that can be added to program backlogs for future releases.

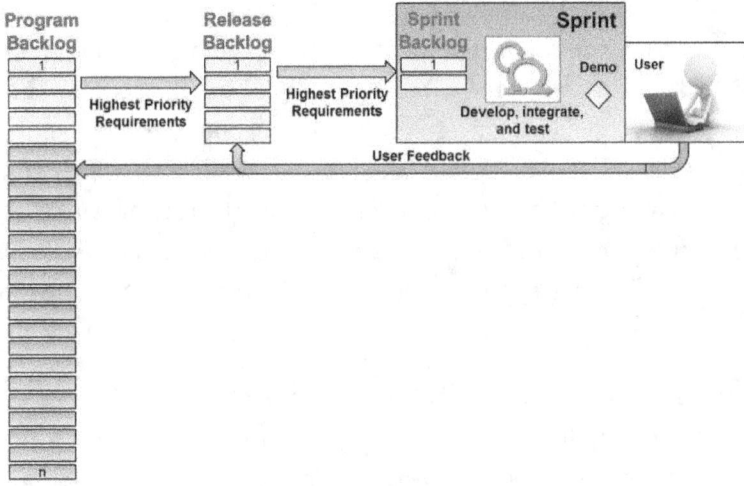

Figure 5. Agile Requirements Process

For more information on Agile Requirements, see:

- Agile Requirements Best Practices by Scott Ambler
- Agile Requirements Change Management by Scott Ambler
- Agile Requirements Modeling by Scott Ambler
- Agile Software Requirements: Lean Requirements Practices for Teams, Programs, and the Enterprise by Dean Leffingwell

1.3.2 Develop, Integrate, and Test Capabilities via Releases and Sprints

Although terminology and timelines may vary in Agile development methods, the foundation is built around small, frequent capability releases. For the purposes of this guide, the following structure will be used to convey the concepts. Programs are able to tailor terms and timelines, as necessary, based on operational environment, developer environment, team velocity, contracting and testing timelines, budgets, and other factors.

- Release—A six-month effort that includes design, development, integration, test, certification, and delivery of capabilities to the users. It is comprised of multiple sprints.
- Sprint—A one-month effort whereby the developer designs, develops, integrates, tests, and demonstrates a set of capabilities to the government. In some instances (e.g., patch for an IA issue), sprints may be fielded, but in most cases, they are interim development efforts.

Planning efforts will be conducted prior to each release and sprint. Release planning is done at a strategic, high level often considering which user stories (requirements) to include in the release. It is conducted after the product backlog has been developed or groomed. It outlines intent, not a firm commitment, and the scope may be revised after each sprint. Sprint planning goes into more tactical-level details. The developers commit to a specific set of user stories to complete in the sprint.

Development, integration, and testing are conducted iteratively throughout the sprint, often with daily integration and automated testing. The core team will consist of staff from the contractor and government. Requirements owners should be actively involved throughout the development phase to clarify requirements, convey the concepts of operation, and provide immediate feedback on interim developments. At the end of each sprint, the developers demonstrate the capability to the government stakeholders to include the requirements owner, testers, certifiers, systems engineers, and program manager. Feedback is provided to the developers, and changes are captured on the program and/or release backlogs.

A release will consist of multiple sprints. The timing of each will depend on many factors, including but not limited to operational need, development risk, contracting timelines, and resource availability. Following a planning phase of a month, a six-month release can include five monthly sprints, with the last month dedicated to operational testing and certifications. At the end of each sprint, as part of the demonstration, the contractor could deliver interim capabilities to the government. Government testers, certifiers, users, engineers, and others could review the interim capabilities to test completeness, identify any issues, and provide feedback to the contractor in parallel to their continued development. A collaborative environment and tools are required for this to be effective.

A completed Integrated Checklist is required for entrance to an Operational Test Readiness Review and to subsequently enter the Operations and Sustainment Phase. The program/project manager is responsible for ensuring that the checklist is completed; however, the individual responses and data entry will likely involve collaboration across many communities. This effort is known as the self-

assessment phase because the program is reporting about itself. The Integrated Checklist is located (currently not available at the time of publication).

Validation of the adapted COTS/GOTS products using an approved test plan is required to obtain network certification and add the products to the Service Catalog. A network certification is obtained through a knowledge point review and documented in a decision memorandum that the DA approves.

1.3.3 Agile Testing

For Agile Development Programs, some version of the following T&E steps should be implemented.

1) Prior to Decision Point 2, develop an evaluation framework that covers the high-level mission objectives for the program. This includes the Critical Operational Issues (COIs) and test measures that address the mission activities supported by the program's capabilities, the sustainment/suitability aspects, security, and interoperability. At this level, the test measures are "solution agnostic" in that they focus on measuring the extent that operational tasks and activities can be accomplished, regardless of the technical implementation that is used to accomplish them. (Example of a mission-based activity: Identify all aircraft repair facilities in a particular region.)

2) In support of Decision Point 2, develop a test strategy or T&E Management Plan, to describe the approach for answering the test measures. Some test measures will be answered directly during test (e.g., performance/capability), while others may be answered through continuous monitoring after fielding (e.g., availability, reliability, service desk). Describe how emerging user requirements (a.k.a., User Stories) for each release will be incorporated into the evaluation framework, and how the intended series of sprint and release-level test events will collectively answer the evaluation framework. Clearly describe if test reporting will focus solely on each release's new content, or if reporting must also cover the program as a whole (i.e., old, unchanged content as well as the new). Discuss how risk assessments will be used in the determination of how much testing is required for each release. Risk assessments should consider the likelihood of failure and impact on mission to appropriately determine the scope of testing required (see Chapter IV).

3) For each release, tailor the evaluation framework as necessary to cover each User Story being targeted by the release and develop a risk assessment. The risk assessment should describe the type of testing and/or test conditions needed to mitigate each risk area (i.e., a purely technical change/enhancement may be adequately validated by functional lab testing, whereas a new capability or user-impacting change may necessitate having an operational user exercising the capability in an operational context in order to validate).

4) Execute testing.

5) In support of Decision Point D, report the test results. Report should cover the status of each User Story, regression test results (new features did/did not break existing functionality), problem reports, and the overall operational effectiveness, suitability, interoperability, and security determinations. Interoperability certification should also be issued at this time.

For additional information on testing and network certification, reference Chapter IV, Section 10. For additional information on testing in Agile development, reference:

- Test and Evaluation for Agile IT by Dr. Steve Hutchinson
- Shift Left by Dr. Steve Hutchinson, Defense AT&L Magazine
- Agile Testing Strategies by Scott Ambler and Associates
- Agile Testing Strategies by Scott Ambler on Dr. Dobbs
- Agile Testing: A Practical Guide for Testers and Agile Teams by Lisa Crispin and Janet Gregory

1.3.4 Continual Technology Development (Pilots/Prototypes)

The acquisition team should continue piloting/prototyping activities conducted in the Design Phase.

For additional information on Continual Technology Development, reference Chapter IV, Section 9.

1.3.5 Refine and Update Strategies, Baselines, and Processes

Throughout the Development, Integration, and Test phase, the acquisition team should embrace a continual process improvement culture. Central to agile methodologies are retrospectives at the end of each sprint and release to identify what worked, what didn't work, and how the team can improve in future efforts. The various acquisition, contracting, systems engineering, test, and other strategies and processes should be tweaked along the way to optimize performance, quality, and capability deliveries while decreasing costs, schedule, and risks. Active collaboration across the team and with external stakeholders across the enterprise is critical. The team must stay attuned to evolution of the enterprise architecture, changes to DISA's enterprise business model, operational experience, and feedback from customers about capabilities delivered to date and capability demands still unmet.

The technical, cost, and performance baselines must be kept current and synchronized to enable an awareness of current status and effectively plan or respond to changes going forward. Affordability assessments, tradeoff analyses, pricing strategies, and performance optimization can be achieved.

1.4 Deployment Decision(s)

Deployment Decisions(s) by the Decision Authority will review the testing and certification reports to verify that the program meets performance requirements, validate that the capabilities meet the operational sponsor/enterprise's needs, and ensure that there is a sound strategy to operate, maintain, support, and evolve the capability.

In addition to the key questions identified above, the acquisition team should be prepared to answer the following standard questions at Deployment Decision(s):

Standard Questions for Deployment Decisions:
• Has sufficient testing been conducted on the program?
• Do test results show the program is suitable and effective?
• Has the program been independently validated and verified?

- Has the program completed the required elements of the integrated checklist?
- Does the program have a suitable plan to operate and sustain the capabilities with appropriate IA?
- Does the program have a suitable plan to provide patches, upgrades, and additional releases?
- Does the program have sufficient budget to meet estimated operational and sustainment costs?
- Does the organization responsible for the operating the capability concur with deployment?
- Do the appropriate stakeholders agree that the capability is ready to be deployed?

In addition, the following information is required for Deployment Decision approval:

Information Required at Deployment Decision(s):
- Updated Acquisition Strategy (includes Lifecycle Sustainment Plan, Information Assurance Strategy, Technical Data Rights Strategy, Information Support Plan, Item Unique Identifier Plan, Performance Management Strategy, Transition to DECC, and Support Posture)
- Operational Test and Evaluation Results
- Updated Services Operations Annex
- Integrated Checklist
- Joint Interoperability Test Command (JITC) Certification
- Clinger-Cohen Act Compliance
- Acquisition Lessons Learned and Best Practices
- Authorization to Operate (ATO)

1.5 Operations and Support

The objectives of the operations and support phase are to operate and support the capability for the user through the end of the intended lifecycle. In an agile environment, after a capability is fielded, updates and enhancements can be made either via a small patch, a new sprint, or new increment. Small patches are made to address a critical deficiency, particularly for information assurance. These are small in scope and schedule but still require proper coordination with information assurance and other certification officials, as well as approval via the operational change management process, prior to installing in an operational environment. Most of the time, the deficiency is captured in a program backlog and integrated into a future sprint or release. Although most sprints are for development only, they could be deployed before the full release is completed, based on operational and programmatic risk, with sufficient coordination and approval.

In addition to operating the service for the user, acquisition planning for technical refresh, modernization, and/or follow-on activities begins in this phase. Analysis of subsequent requirements across the DISA portfolios should be conducted to ensure that efforts are not duplicated and that the best approach is identified. If a refresh or follow-on activity is not required, the phase concludes with a decision for project disposal.

During the Operations and Support phase, the capability will be operated using the operational processes defined in the Defense Enterprise Service Management Framework (DESMF). Depending on

the agreed operational concept documented as part of the Service Operations Framework, the acquisition organization may have enduring responsibilities for providing on-call technical expertise to help resolve escalated operational issues.

For more information on Operation and Sustainment, see Chapter IV, Section 12

1.6 Model Variations

The agile development model can be further tailored for several development efforts, as shown in Table 3.

Table 3. Agile Development Model Variations

Model Variation	Design	Development, Integration, and Test
DoD unique software delivered via multiple short releases (based on finite set of requirements)	After some initial design and architecture, most design efforts done at release level.	Iterative development via monthly sprints and 6–12 month releases to users. Max use of automated tests.
Small DoD unique application	Rapid if leveraging existing design standards, interfaces, infrastructure, and processes.	Small development team commensurate with scope. Max use of automated tests.
Minor enhancements or maintenance to an existing program	Limited design and docs as minimal scope of work and leveraging established program.	Ideally leverages existing contract with developer. Requires upfront agreement on testing and IA required.
Major enhancements to an existing program	Requires most activities and docs to capture scope and plan to build on program.	Development similar to follow-on release of agile or incremental program.

1.7 Additional Agile References

- Manifesto for Agile Software Development
- MITRE Handbook for Implementing Agile in DoD IT Acquisition
- Software Engineering Institute: Considerations for Using Agile in DoD Acquisition
- Software Engineering Institute: Agile Methods: Selected DoD Management and Acquisition Concerns
- GAO Report 12-681 Effective Practices and Federal Challenges in Applying Agile Methods.

2 Incremental Development (Model 2)

The incremental development model is used for the development of DoD unique hardware and software applications often via one or more larger increments of capabilities. The program often includes software development and/or infrastructure design and development. This model is appropriate for major programs for which the deployment and operational user community are significantly impacted by new capability delivery.

This model is applied when larger increments of capability delivery are appropriate. Examples include delivery of new increments that require significant changes to infrastructure, operational processes, and TTPs. Another example includes capabilities, such as enterprise services, that have a large user base and ongoing deployments/migrations for which delivery of new capabilities impacts adoption.

As illustrated in Figure 6, this model closely follows the traditional acquisition models in DoDI 5000.02. The draft update to DoDI 5000.02 in 2013 has models for Hardware Intensive, Defense Unique Software Intensive, and Incrementally Fielded Software Intensive programs, and for Hybrid options. Acquisition teams using this acquisition model should use the DoDI 5000.02 models as the foundation and reference Chapter IV of this guide for DISA tailoring of individual processes.

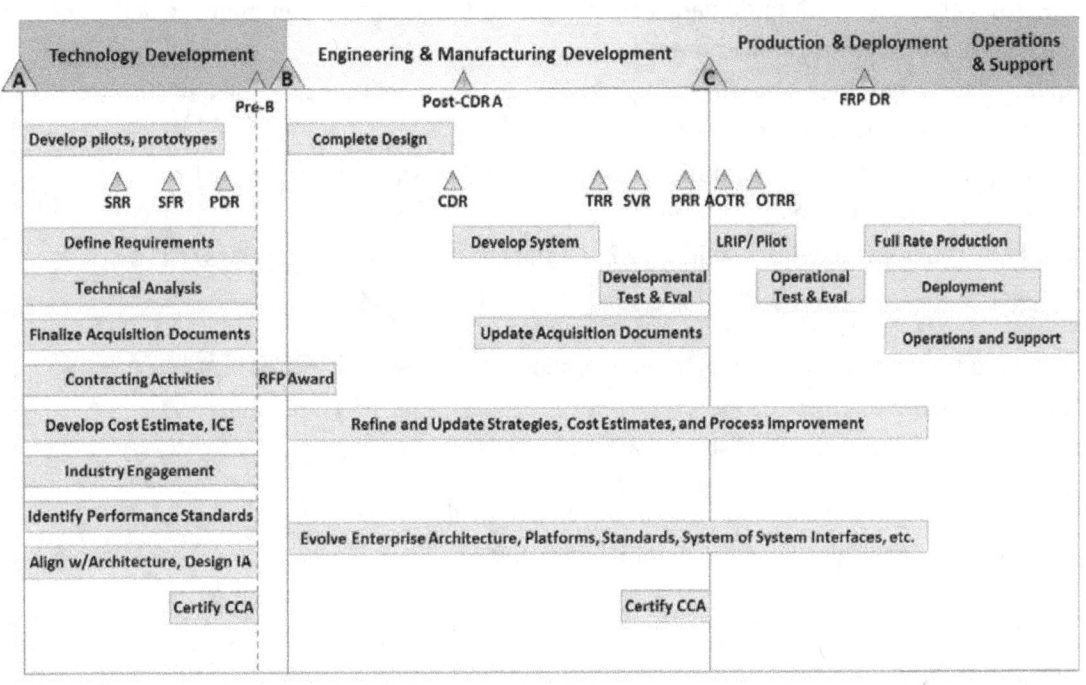

Figure 6. Incremental Development Model Process View

2.1   Program Structure

A critical element of the program structure model is effectively structuring the program using increments or related elements. The structure will play a key role in shaping the acquisition strategy and risk with significant impacts to the program's success. DoD IT programs have struggled to effectively deliver capabilities in the acquisition framework designed for large weapon systems. According to the Defense Science Board, IT acquisition programs originally structured as five-year increments actually delivered capabilities on average of 81 months. Given the dynamic, rapidly evolving pace of change in IT, speed to delivery is a critical aspect. When determining the scope and length of the increments, the acquisition team must consider:

- **Technology maturity**— Does the current increment use mature technology? Can immature technologies be reserved for subsequent increments?
- **Risk**—What are the operational, technical, programmatic, schedule, and cost risks?
- **Complexity**—Should the increment be kept small to reduce the complexity? Does the system design require a major, complex element that requires a longer timeframe?
- **Integration**—What is the level of integration required for subsystems, COTS/GOTS, enterprise infrastructure, and related systems and platforms?
- **Urgency**—What are the warfighter demands and timelines? Can a partial solution be fielded ASAP and evolve with subsequent increments?
- **Cost and budget**—Is the increment affordable? Smaller scoped increments should have higher fidelity cost estimates and budget stability.
- **Performance priorities**—Does the operational environment demand a minimum performance level? Examine threshold vs. objective levels.
- **Contracting**—What are the contract limitations? Can the contract include incentives to drive faster delivery?

As speed to delivery is often the primary driver, increments should be scoped accordingly. Acquisition teams and PEOs should explore use of capstone documents, processes, contracts, and related resources to enable faster timelines and consistent practices.

Detailed processes for this model will be provided in a subsequent guidebook version. If using this model, refer to the Defense Acquisition Guidebook for instructions.

2.2   Test and Evaluation for Incrementally Developed Programs

For incrementally developed programs, the traditional processes, documents, and events as described in DoD 5000.02 and the Defense Acquisition Guide should be used. If on OSD oversight, attention must be paid to additional staffing and timelines imposed by DDTE and DOT&E. A summary of the key T&E activities are:

1) Form an integrated test team via the T&E WIPT consisting of all the testing stakeholders, including representatives from a cross-section of the intended user population.

42

2) Create an evaluation framework consisting of COIs and associated test measures to define how the program will be evaluated for Operational Effectiveness, Suitability, Interoperability, and Security (OESIS). Ideally, all the data needed by the testing stakeholders will be covered by the single evaluation framework (e.g., data needed for interoperability certification is covered by effectiveness test measures for information exchanges, and by suitability test measures for the ability to enter and be managed in the intended network).

3) In support of Milestone B, the T&E WIPT creates a T&E Master Plan (TEMP) to describe the test regimen used, the operational conditions and factors covered/not covered by testing, the roles and responsibilities of all testing stakeholders, the risk assessment process to be used, and the resources required to fully execute the TEMP. The TEMP is normally revised to support Milestone C, as well.

4) Based on a risk assessment, design and execute test events to generate the required test data under the appropriate conditions, while minimizing duplication of efforts. Likely, the test regimen will include events in both laboratory and operational environments.

5) At Milestone C, test results to date conclude readiness for Operational Testing (OT), interoperability status, and illuminate any remaining risks in support of a limited fielding decision.

6) Post Milestone C, dedicated OT is conducted to the extent necessary.

7) Final reporting includes determinations for Operational Effectiveness, Suitability, Interoperability, and Security. All interoperability requirements have been tested and the Interoperability Certification is issued. Final reporting supports the Full Fielding Decision Review (FFDR).

For additional information on testing and network certification, reference Chapter IV, Section 10.

DISA IT Acquisition Guidebook

3 Defense Business Systems (Model 3)

Development or customization of COTS software for DoD business processes. Processes conform to the DoD Business Capability Lifecycle (BCL). The model in Figure 7 has been adapted from the DoD BCL.

Some of the key characteristics of this acquisition model include:

- Identifying the customer base for the acquisition and developing a process to obtain continuous customer involvement in the ongoing requirements documentation and prioritization process.
- Assessing current interface standards and interface technology for the development of the interface requirements and design.
- Development of a data management strategy to include data conversion and records management.
- Strategy for capacity/scalability management.
- Strategy to define and predict performance under peak loads.

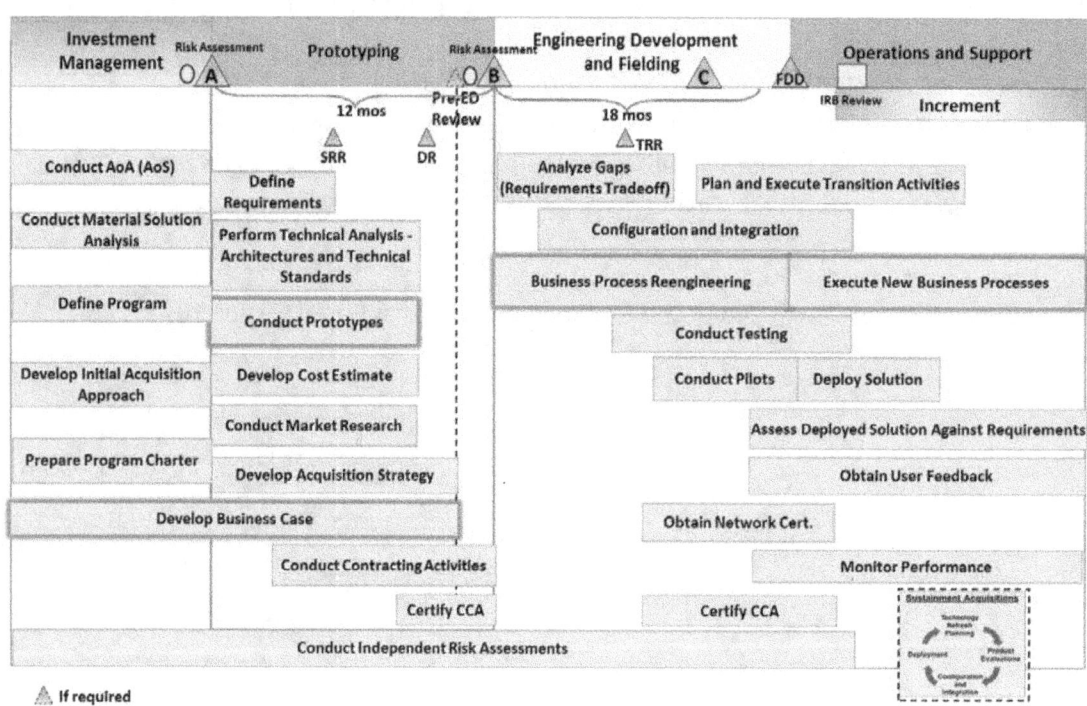

Figure 7 Defense Business Systems Model Process View

3.1 Prototyping Phase

The requirements are refined and finalized in the prototyping phase using the analyses of alternatives from the investment management phase (referred to as the initiation phase in this guide). Acquisition

44

teams using this acquisition model should use BCL as the foundation and reference Chapter IV of this guide for DISA tailoring of individual processes.

3.2 Milestone B

At Milestone B the Decision Authority reviews analyses and strategies to develop the capabilities, ensures that the design integrates mature technologies aligned to enterprise architectures, and verifies program affordability to meet validated requirements within the available budget. The Decision Authority approves the release of the RFP or contract award at Milestone B.

In addition to the key questions identified above, the acquisition team should be prepared to answer the following standard questions at Milestone B.

Key Questions for Prototyping Phase:

- Who is the customer base for the requirement?
- How is the customer involved in the ongoing requirements documentation and prioritization process?
- Have current interface standards and interface technology been assessed and factored into the development of the interface requirements and the feasible design?
- What is the data management strategy to include data conversion and records management?
- Is there a capacity/scalability management strategy and plan?
- How is performance under peak loads defined and predicted?
- What is the business model for establishing the cost and pricing strategy to recover investment costs as well as the ongoing O&M costs?
- Has a customer relationship management (CRM) strategy been incorporated into the acquisition strategy and deployment plan? Have appropriate CRM processes been established?
- What is the deployment plan to get to the target solution?
- Have SLAs been established to manage customer relationships?
- Have current interface standards and interface technology been assessed and factored into the development of the interface requirements and the feasible design?
- What is the strategy for incorporating newer versions of technologies?
- How long will the vendor support and maintain older software versions?
- What is the approach for providing tiered-level of technical customer support?
- Does the design integrate mature technologies and align to DISA architectures, standards, and interfaces?
- Does the design anticipate technological evolution?
- Does the design consider Mission Assurance?
- Is the product/service a candidate for a DISA standard processing environment (e.g., RACE, FORGE.mil)?
- Are the resources requirements for the DISA standard processing environment and the associated migration activities adequately addressed in the acquisition strategy?

- If the product/service is not a candidate for the standard processing environment, has a waiver been obtained?
- Does the strategy plan specify the use of DISA standardized Service Operations tools (e.g. for pro-active monitoring, service-level compliance, and trouble-ticketing)?
- Does the strategy plan specify the operations functions that will support the capability (e.g. cognizant Service Desk, Technical Management, IT Operations Management, and Access Management teams) and how they will be resourced?
- Does the program have sufficient systems engineering processes, reviews?
- Is there a change management process for design and requirements changes?
- Is there a technical baseline for the program?
- Has a sufficient technical/cost tradeoff analysis been conducted?
- Have post-deployment operational costs over the full lifecycle been included in cost estimates?

Standard Questions for Milestone B:
- Are the program requirements validated and prioritized?
- Have rigorous cost estimates been conducted?
- Is the program affordable within the available budget?
- Does the contract strategy address risk, incentives, data rights, and competition across the lifecycle?
- Does the team actively engage industry to shape strategy?
- Is testing integrated and scaled based on program risk?
- Is there a transition plan to deploy capabilities?
- Is there a plan to operate the capability in accordance with the DISA Service Operations Framework?
- Is there a realistic Integrated Master Schedule?
- Has the program identified and mitigated risks?
- Does the strategy satisfy the customer's requirements?
- Is the strategy designed to maximize competition?
- How will the contract type minimize risk to the government?
- Are there existing contract vehicles available for the required services? If not, should DISA develop an enterprise contract vehicle for this service?
- Does the strategy appropriately leverage contract type and objective incentives to motivate contractors to exceed minimum performance requirements?
- Have conflict-of-interest issues been addressed and eliminated or mitigation plans established?

The following information is also required for Milestone B approval:

Required at Milestone B:

- Acquisition Strategy (includes Technical Analysis, Market Research, Pilot/Prototype Results, Information Support Plan, Technical Data Rights Strategy, Systems Engineering Plan, Architecture Strategy, Test and Evaluation Management Plan, and Lifecycle Sustainment Plan)
- Capability Requirements Document
- Concept of Operations
- Services Operations Annex
- Acquisition Program Baseline
- Lifecycle Cost Estimate
- Acquisition Plan
- Request for Proposal and Other Contracting Docs
- Service Level Agreements (when applicable)
- Business Processes Reengineering (when applicable)
- Clinger-Cohen Act Compliance

The acquisition team will prepare an Acquisition Decision Memorandum (ADM) and the Decision Authority will sign it. The ADM will capture the key decisions in the meeting, any action items for the acquisition team, and any guidance or deviations from policy and guidance for criteria for the next acquisition phase and deployment decision.

3.3 Engineering Development and Fielding Phase

BCL provides high-level guidance on the activities that need to be conducted in this phase. The acquisition team should also refer to Chapter IV for additional information on key process activities for this model.

3.4 Milestone C

Milestone C deployment decisions(s) by the Decision Authority will review the testing and certification reports to verify the program meets performance requirements, validate that the capabilities meet the operational sponsor/ enterprise's needs, and ensure there is a sound strategy to operate, maintain, support, and evolve the capability.

The acquisition team should be prepared to answer the standard questions at Milestone C.

Standard Questions for Milestone C:
- Has sufficient testing been conducted on the program?
- Do test results show the program is suitable and effective?
- Has the program been independently validated and verified?
- Has the program completed the required elements of the integrated checklist?
- Does the program have a suitable plan to operate and sustain the capabilities w/appropriate IA?
- Does the program have a suitable plan to provide patches, upgrades, and additional releases?
- Does the program have sufficient budget to meet estimated operational and sustainment costs?

- Does the organization responsible for operating the capability concur with deployment?
- Do the appropriate stakeholders agree the capability is ready to be deployed?

Additionally, the following information is required for Milestone C approval:

Information Required at Milestone C:
- Updated Acquisition Strategy (includes: Lifecycle Sustainment Plan, Information Assurance Strategy, Technical Data Rights Strategy, Information Support Plan, Item Unique Identifier Plan, Performance Management Strategy, Transition to DECC, and Support Posture)
- Operational Test and Evaluation Results
- Current Risk Adjusted Lifecycle Cost Estimate
- Updated Services Operations Annex
- Integrated Checklist
- JITC Certification
- Clinger-Cohen Act Compliance
- Acquisition Lessons Learned and Best Practices
- Authorization to Operate (ATO)

3.5 Operations and Support Phase

BCL provides high-level guidance on the activities that need to be conducted in this phase. The acquisition team should also refer to Chapter IV for additional information on key process activities for this model.

DISA IT Acquisition Guidebook

4 IT Commodities (Model 4)

The IT commodities model (Figure 8) is used to acquire COTS/GOTS hardware and software products (non-developmental items) that provide needed functionality "out-of-the-box." Modifications are acceptable when they are of a type customarily available in the commercial marketplace or are minor modifications that do not alter the nongovernmental function or essential physical characteristics of an item or component. A service is also considered a commercial item when it is of a type offered and sold competitively in substantial quantities in the commercial market on the basis of established catalog or market prices for specific tasks performed under standard commercial terms and conditions.

Some of the key characteristics of this acquisition model include:

- Consideration for enterprise strategy sourcing initiatives.
- Strategy to maximize volume discounts.
- Identification of certifications that maximize the reuse potential from other organizations.
- Strategy to address implementation and maintenance based on the frequency of vendor/contractor release cycles.
- Strategy for incorporating new versions of technologies.

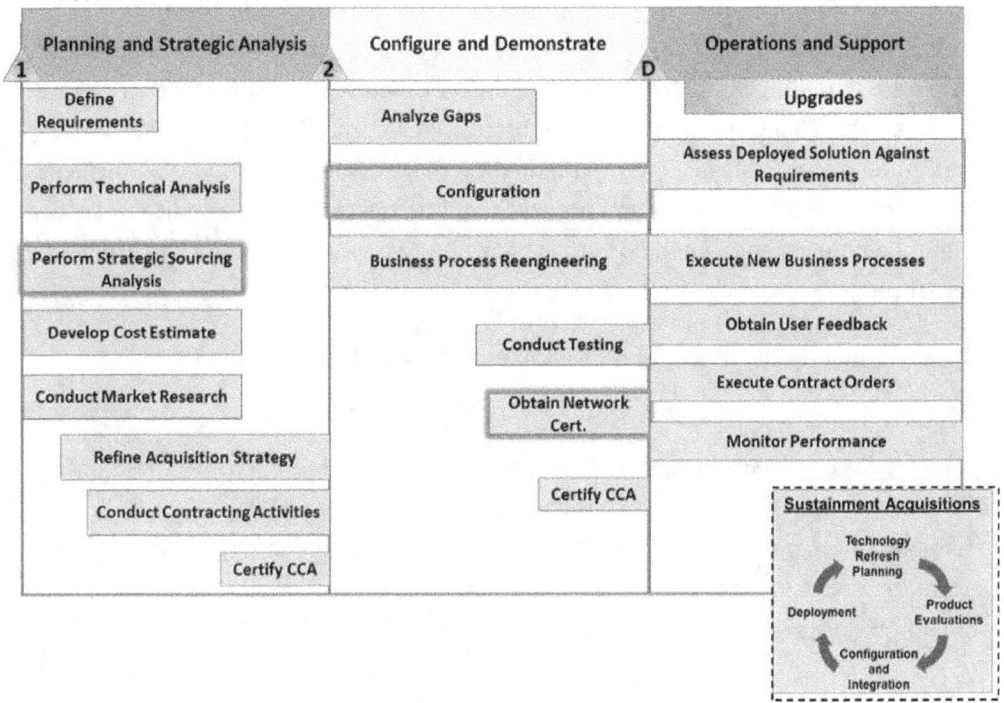

Figure 8 IT Commodities Model Process View

4.1 Planning and Strategic Analysis Phase

Activities to be performed in the planning and strategic analysis phase continue building on the documents and decisions from the initiation phase. The requirements are refined and finalized in this

49

phase using the analyses of alternatives from the initiation phase. The activities in this phase—shaping requirements, conducting technical analysis of COTS/GOTS, and conducting strategic sourcing analysis, cost estimates, market research, contracting, etc.—are performed in parallel and tightly aligned. All of the processes influence each other and will help the acquisition team develop the optimal strategy for the acquisition.

The following activities, documents, and plans must be executed, developed, and completed/approved.

4.1.1 Define Requirements

In concert with the analysis and strategies in this phase, the acquisition team will refine and finalize the requirements to effectively baseline and acquire the capabilities.

All members of the acquisition team should be strongly engaged in the requirements definition process, especially the requirements (user) community. Defining requirements begins with the drafting of a statement of the user's need, including the level of performance and availability the end-user would like to have. This statement should define the operational need for the item, including the intended use, and should also define the desired support services, such as training, testing, maintenance, and repair services.

As the process to refine requirements continues, logistics support that could impact the requirements should also be considered. Additionally, factors such as product availability and upgrade plans, as well as customary warranty and reliability assurances, should be considered and their impact appropriately discussed in the acquisition planning stage. The clear definition of hardware and software interfaces is another factor to consider in developing requirements and acquisition strategies. Periodically, software interfaces may need to be redesigned to keep up with evolving commercial technology and improve total system performance.

For additional information on requirements, reference Chapter IV, Section 1.

> **Key Questions:**
> - What general capabilities are available in the marketplace to satisfy the requirement?
> - Can commercial items or modified commercial items satisfy the requirement?
> - How can the basic requirements statement be refined to maximize the benefit of competitive market forces and the use of commercial items without increasing the potential for product failure and/or greater lifecycle costs?

4.1.2 Perform Technical Analysis

A comprehensive technical analysis is probably one of the most important aspects of this acquisition model. This requires extensive analysis of existing COTS and GOTS products, the technical environment they must operate in, and their ability to meet the user requirements to accomplish their mission objectives. This is a dynamic set of tradeoffs between the three elements.

The team should begin with an initial set of requirements to meet the mission objectives to provide an initial scope. These requirements and scope will likely adjust based on the technical analysis. Often the users' interest in an existing COTS/GOTS product may be the initial driver for the acquisition.

The team will identify, benchmark, and analyze viable COTS/GOTS products using the results of market research. This includes first-hand analysis from systems engineering, information assurance, and users' perspectives. The team can also leverage any independent analysis of commercial products conducted by industry experts. A side-by-side comparison of key features, costs, risks, IA, usability, integration, scalability, compatibility with DISA standard management tools, and related factors should be compiled. During the analysis, some products may be deemed nonviable by not meeting basic standards. The team can focus their analysis on the remaining ones, essentially down-selecting along the way to a suitable number to select from. Options may include different combinations of COTS/GOTS products.

The technical analysis should investigate the design, security, integration, support, performance, and other elements of the COTS/GOTS software. Software Questionnaires are available containing over 50 questions for the acquisition teams to consider for COTS, GOTS, Open Source Software, Custom Software, and Hosted Applications. Please contact the CAE for copies of the questionnaires.

The technical environment must be clearly understood. It should comply with DISA's Enterprise Architectures, and the team should actively collaborate with the Chief Engineers Panel (CEP) and other architecture owners (e.g., DISA EE3). The acquisition strategy should clearly identify points in the process where the program will consult with the CEP. Each viable product should be assessed as to how it would fit and operate within the architecture. DISA (or another DoD organization) may have already certified some products for Information Assurance. Reciprocity should be leveraged to the maximum extent to avoid duplicative and lengthy certifications.

A thorough technical analysis should include review of existing DISA architectures, technical standards, and IT platforms from the perspectives of interoperability, integration, technology maturity, and evolution strategy. Verification and validation criteria regarding the ability of the acquired products to meet the functional objectives should also be considered in this step. The analysis should be performed with the CEP to ensure compliance with the DISA Enterprise Architecture. For more information on DISA's Enterprise Architecture, visit CEP.

Key Questions:
- What kind of certifications will maximize reuse potential?
- What are the common standards and security requirements for the enterprise?
- Does the design consider Mission Assurance?
- Is there a comprehensive, complete, current, and independently reviewed technical baseline that aligns to cost, requirements, budget, schedule, enterprise architectures?

4.1.3 Conduct Market Research

The acquisition team should continue with the market research that was conducted in the initiation phase.

Product evaluation is a critical element of this phase, and active industry engagement can be an invaluable part of the process. Through market research and industry engagement, the acquisition team should have a list of potential COTS/GOTS solutions. This candidate list will often offer a wide variety of features, capabilities, risks, and opportunities. The evaluation of candidate products will help shape the final requirements and scope of the program or project. As the acquisition team performs the technical analysis, they should actively engage industry to identify and understand COTS product features, ratings, costs, risks, and more. Collaborating with independent experts who review these products is another valuable source of information to product selection. Industry engagement must be done in accordance with the contracting officer's guidance.

The acquisition team is also encouraged to use a Request for Information (RFI) or use an industry day to understand the breadth and depth of capabilities available in the marketplace to fulfill the government needs.

A summary of the market research should be included in the acquisition strategy and any relevant acquisition plan.

For additional information on market research, reference Chapter IV, Section 6.2.

4.1.4 Perform Strategic Sourcing Analysis

Strategic sourcing is a proven best practice that promotes a systematic and collaborative approach to sourcing supplies. It is the process of critically analyzing an organization's spending and using this information to make business decisions about acquiring commodities and services more effectively and efficiently. It represents a shift from buying tactically, on an as-needed basis, to buying collaboratively, with well-planned service acquisitions that consider spending trends and future requirements of the entire enterprise. Strategic sourcing is applying the *best* approach to spending money. strategic sourcing benefits include:

- Increased collaboration and communication
- Enhanced supplier relationships and market expertise
- Improved holistic views of Defense-wide requirements
- Increased workforce skills, efficiency, and effectiveness
- Increased understanding of small business spend and markets
- Standardized business processes
- Maintained workforce balance
- Reduced number of duplicative business arrangements
- Reduced duplication of effort

Strategic sourcing improves the transparency of requirements across the Defense Enterprise and reduces redundant business arrangements. Commodity COTS/GOTS acquisitions can benefit from effective and efficient sourcing strategies to gain cost and schedule benefits by leveraging the agency's and the department's buying power to obtain lower prices through volume discounts and increase buying efficiencies.

When acquiring an IT commodity, the acquisition team should always consider if the commodity should be made available for DISA or DoD-wide use via a strategic sourcing contract vehicle. Not only do strategic sourcing contracts provide greater cost savings by leveraging the buying power of the department, they can also provide significant time savings for future orders of the IT commodity. The acquisition team should engage with PLD as early as possible when considering this strategy. Strategic sourcing begins during acquisition strategy formulation when requirements are identified. The team should review past and present business arrangements, review industry trends and qualified suppliers, conduct a total cost of ownership analysis, and consolidate the results to develop a sourcing strategy.

Spend analysis is the foundation for identifying strategic sourcing focus areas. A spend analysis assesses the breakdown of spending in terms of:

- Who did the buying? (Contracting Agency)
- Who did the spending? (Requesting Agency)
- How much was spent?
- What type of contract award was used? (Blanket Purchase Agreement, Purchase Order, Delivery Order, Definitive Contract)
- What was purchased? (Portfolio Groups/FSC/PSC)
- What was the size of the purchase? (>$1M, <$1M, Micro Purchase threshold, etc.)
- What acquisition method was used? (Assisted vs. Direct)
- What type of contract was used? (Cost, Firm Fixed Price, Time & Materiel, etc.)
- Who received the work? (Top 1%, Top 10, Top 100)

Strategic sourcing must be performed continuously to understand the constant changes in organizational spending—both past and future. It not only addresses actions leading to contract award, but actions and spending taking place after contract award. Strategic sourcing activities are accomplished early so as to shape and influence the development and approval of the individual contract acquisition strategy—especially as it relates to the sourcing decision. Strategic sourcing solutions can range from implementing supplier partnerships, to establishing centers of excellence (based on region or core competencies), to leveraging strategic business arrangements that garner results for the enterprise. By creating an environment of data transparency and instilling a culture of strategic decision making and collaboration, the department can provide strategically sourced goods and services that maximize procurement dollars, resources, and warfighter support. Strategic sourcing seeks to maximize enterprise-level benefits by achieving for the warfighter the right balance in terms of

product/service quality and innovation, delivery time, prices, competition, contract administration costs and workload, and socio-economic goals.

Figure 9 provides the strategic sourcing framework promulgated by Defense Procurement and Acquisition Policy, Strategic Sourcing. For more information on strategic sourcing, visit the DPAP website.

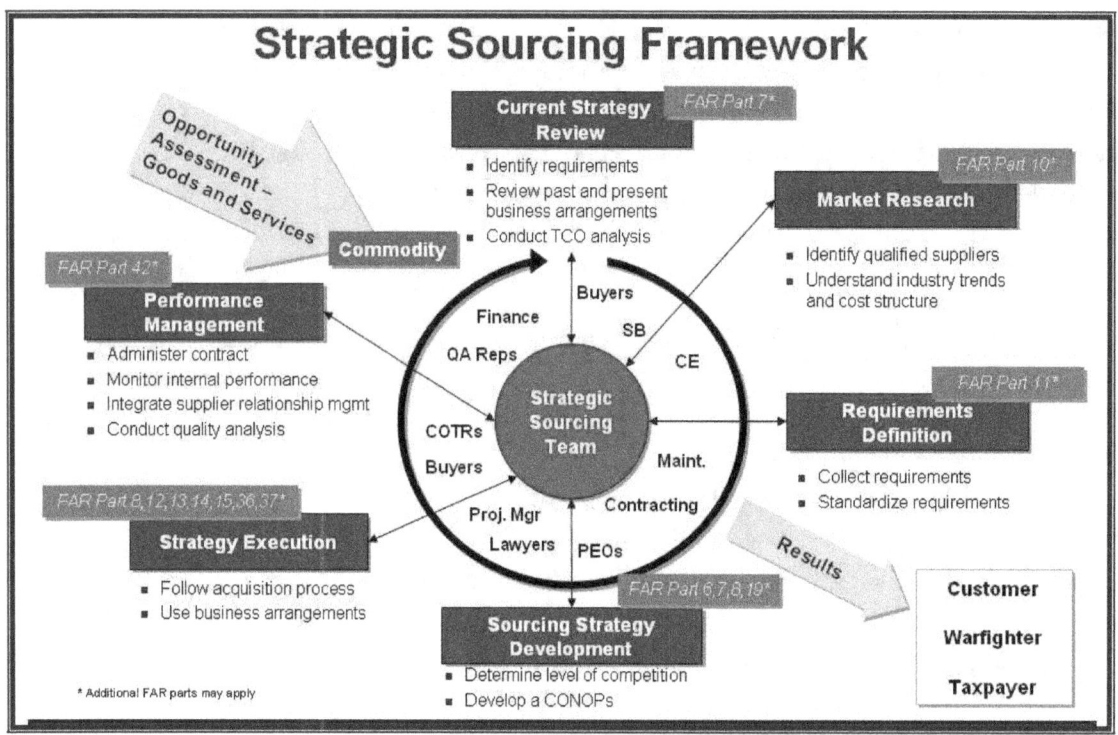

Figure 9 Strategic Sourcing Framework (Source: DPAP)

Key Questions:
- Should these commodities be acquired as part of an enterprise strategic sourcing initiative?
- Have volume discounts been considered and at what quantity can discounts be maximized?

4.1.5 Develop Cost Estimate

Once the acquisition team identifies that suitable commercial products or services are available in the marketplace to meet the government's need, the government should use commercially available pricing information for the cost estimate. An important aspect of the cost estimate is the consideration of lifecycle costs, including configuration control and logistics support. The degrees of contractor configuration control and logistics support should relate to total cost, performance, and risk. This is critical because the government does not control how the vendor schedules and manages releases/version, that could adversely impact the systems with which it interfaces. The management

structure, including the costs of managing change (both the design aspects as well as potentially supporting multiple configurations), must be considered.

The use of commercial products or components also requires lifecycle planning for change, and this should be incorporated in the cost estimate. Carefully consider the possibility, and associated costs, of any custom integration software that may be required to ensure legacy programs will operate with and on any new hardware and software upgrades. For example, when the vendor updates their operating system, which the government has elected to use, not all programs procured through a different vendor may be necessarily operating on a plug-and-play basis. Integration or "glue" code may need to be developed and maintained. The cost estimate must also include any annual licensing fees for COTS software. Technology refresh and/or upgrades and the associated intervals should be considered and included. It must include planning for technology refreshment and maintaining any associated software after production. This includes how changes (for obsolescence/ technology refreshment and maintaining the software) will be budgeted and executed along with the necessary technical data required to sustain the system throughout the lifecycle.

For additional information on cost estimates, reference Chapter IV, Section 4.

4.1.6 Refine Acquisition Strategy

This activity should build on acquisition strategy developed in the initiation phase and the analysis from this planning and strategic analysis phase. The following factors should be considered in the acquisition strategy:

- Supplier capabilities
- Logistics support
- Product availability
- Technology refreshment (including upgrades, modernization, technology insertion strategies)
- Customary warranty
- Reliability assurances
- Data rights
- Hardware and software interfaces

A technology refreshment strategy ensures systems stay current with the latest commercial technology and when appropriately planned, eliminates or at least reduces total system upgrades. Technology refreshment should be planned and designed into the system early in its life cycle because it will require an Open Systems Architecture design, or commercial standards-based architecture, to maximize COTS "plug and play" refreshments.

For additional information on acquisition strategy, reference Chapter IV, Section 3.

Key Questions:

- Is the product/service a candidate for a DISA standard processing environment (e.g., RACE, FORGE.mil)?
- Are the resources requirements for the DISA standard processing environment and the associated migration activities adequately addressed in the acquisition strategy?
- If the product/service is not a candidate for the standard processing environment, has a waiver been obtained?
- Does the strategy plan specify the use of DISA standardized Service Operations tools (e.g. for pro-active monitoring, service-level compliance, and trouble-ticketing)?
- Does the strategy plan specify the operations functions that will support the capability (e.g. cognizant Service Desk, Technical Management, IT Operations Management, and Access Management teams) and how they will be resourced?
- What is the strategy for incorporating newer versions of technologies?
- What is the technical refresh strategy plan?
- How long will the vendor support and maintain older software versions?

4.1.7 Conduct Contracting Activities

IT Commodity acquisitions are subject to FAR Part 12 commercial contracting procedures. Firm fixed price or fixed-price contracts with economic price adjustments should be used for commercial item acquisitions. The government should take advantage of commercial warranties to the maximum extent practicable. Solicitations should include minimum warranty terms, such as minimum duration, appropriate for the government's intended use of the item.

The program/project office should work with the contracting office as early as possible if considering a strategic sourcing vehicle. Once a strategic sourcing contract is in place, the contracting office can help develop a process to streamline future orders by standardizing processes and implementing the use of contract templates to standardize terms and conditions and business processes. This helps to expedite contracting activities and reduce costs for future commodity orders.

For additional information on contracting, reference Chapter IV, Section 6.

4.1.8 Certify Clinger-Cohen Act

Clinger-Cohen Act (CCA) compliance by DISA CIO is required. For additional information on CCA compliance and certification, reference Chapter IV, Section 8.

4.2 Decision Point 2

At Decision Point 2, the Decision Authority reviews analyses and strategies to acquire the capabilities and verifies program affordability to meet validated requirements within the available budget. The Decision Authority approves the release of the RFP or contract award at Decision Point 2.

In addition to the key questions identified above, the acquisition team should be prepared to answer the following standard questions at Decision Point 2:

56

Standard Questions for Decision Point 2:
- Are the program requirements validated and prioritized?
- Have rigorous cost estimates been conducted?
- Is the program affordable within available budget?
- Does the contract strategy address risk, incentives, data rights, and competition across the lifecycle?
- Does the team actively engage industry to shape strategy?
- Is test integrated and scaled based on program risk?
- Is there a transition plan to deploy capabilities?
- Is there a plan to operate the capability in accordance with the DISA Service Operations Framework?
- Is there a realistic Integrated Master Schedule?
- Has the program identified and mitigated risks?
- Does the strategy satisfy the customer's requirements?
- Is the strategy designed to maximize competition?
- How will the contract type minimize risk to the government?
- Are there existing contract vehicles available for the required services? If not, should DISA develop an enterprise contract vehicle for this service?
- Does the strategy appropriately leverage contract type and objective incentives to motivate contractors to exceed minimum performance requirements?
- Have conflict-of-interest issues been addressed and eliminated or mitigation plans established?

The following information is also required for Decision Point 2 approval:

Information Required at Decision Point 2:
- Acquisition Strategy (includes Technical Analysis, Market Research, Information Support Plan, Technical Data Rights Strategy, Architecture Strategy, and Lifecycle Sustainment Plan)
- Capability Requirements Document
- Concept of Operations
- Services Operations Annex
- Acquisition Program Baseline
- Cost Estimate
- Acquisition Plan
- Request for Proposal and Other Contracting Docs
- Service Level Agreements (when applicable)
- Business Processes Reengineering (when applicable)
- Clinger-Cohen Act Compliance

The acquisition team will prepare an Acquisition Decision Memorandum (ADM) the Decision Authority will sign it. The ADM will capture the key decisions in the meeting, any action items for the acquisition team, and any guidance or deviations from policy and guidance for criteria for the next acquisition phase and deployment decision.

4.3 Configure and Demonstrate Phase

The objectives of the configure and demonstrate phase are to complete the acquisition of the COTS/GOTS products and complete configuration and adapt the product to operate within the DISA enterprise.

Activities to be performed in this phase include performing the configuration of the COTS/GOTS products, testing, and obtaining the necessary certifications and documents to add to the DISA enterprise.

4.3.1 Analyze Gaps

While the team conducted a technical analysis in the previous phase, a gap assessment is needed once the COTS/GOTS products have been acquired. The acquisition team, in collaboration with the contractor and end user, should determine if any gaps exist between the intended functionality of the COTS/GOTS capability and the program needs. If gaps are identified, the acquisition team should consider a variety of options to include alternative technical solutions, business process reengineering, and product customization.

4.3.2 Configuration

This process step may only be required in some cases. The program manager should define configuration management processes to document functional and physical characteristics of the IT commodity products and to establish a technical baseline, if required. Configuration items can consist of the requirements, specifications, hardware, software, and documentation (data). The configuration process also includes documenting all of the necessary functional and physical characteristics of a configuration item; the functional and physical characteristics designated for testing; and identifying the tests necessary for deployment/installation, operation, support, training, and disposal of the configuration item.

4.3.3 Business Process Reengineering

This process step may only be required in some cases. Business Process Reengineering (BPR) is redesigning the way work is done to better support the organization's mission and reduce costs. The intent of BPR in this model is to redesign DISA business processes, to the maximum extent possible, to conform to the best practice business rules adopted by industry. In most cases, it is best to adopt the COTS/GOTS solution "out-of-the-box" rather than adapting the product to accommodate existing systems and processes.

For COTS acquisitions, additional BPR is conducted after program initiation, to reengineer an organization's retained processes to match available COTS processes.

For additional information on BPR, reference Chapter IV, Section 5.

4.3.4 Conduct Testing & Obtain Network Certification

Validation of the acquired IT commodity products using an approved test plan is required to obtain network certification. After completing configuration activities, the government must conduct acceptance and operational testing of the product or service prior to a formal deployment decision. PEO test engineers, JITC testers, and operational user representatives will assess the product or service according to their roles and provide input to the deployment decision.

For additional information on testing, reference Chapter IV, Section 10.

4.3.5 Certify CCA

Clinger-Cohen Act (CCA) compliance by DISA CIO is required. For additional information on CCA compliance and certification, reference Chapter IV, Section 8.

4.4 Deployment Decision(s)

Deployment Decisions(s) by the Decision Authority will review the testing and certification reports to verify that the program meets performance requirements, validate that the capabilities meet the operational sponsor or enterprise's needs, and ensure that there is a sound strategy to operate, maintain, support, and evolve the capability.

The acquisition team should be prepared to answer the following standard questions at Deployment Decision:

Standard Questions for Deployment Decisions:
- Has sufficient testing been conducted on the program?
- Do test results show the program has been implemented based on requirements/customer needs?
- Has the program been independently validated and verified?
- Has the program completed the required elements of the integrated checklist?
- Does the program have a suitable plan to operate and sustain the capabilities with appropriate IA?
- Does the program have a suitable plan to provide patches, upgrades, and additional releases?
- Does the program have sufficient budget to meet estimated operational and sustainment costs?
- Does the organization responsible for operating the capability concur with deployment?
- Do the appropriate stakeholders agree the capability is ready to be deployed?

In addition, the following information is required for Deployment Decision approval:

Information Required at Deployment Decision(s):
- Updated Acquisition Strategy (includes Lifecycle Sustainment Plan, Information Assurance Strategy, Technical Data Rights Strategy, Information Support Plan, Item Unique Identifier Plan, Performance Management Strategy, Transition to DECC, and Support Posture)
- Integrated Checklist
- Updated Services Operations Annex
- Clinger-Cohen Act Compliance

59

- Acquisition Lessons Learned and Best Practices
- Authorization to Operate (ATO)

4.5 Operations and Support Phase

The objectives of the operations and support phase are to operate and support the capability for the user through the end of the intended lifecycle. Considerations for follow-on and/or subsequent technical refresh acquisitions are evaluated in this phase.

During the Operations and Support phase, the capability will be operated using the operational processes defined in the Defense Enterprise Service Management Framework. Depending on the agreed operational concept documented as part of the Service Operations Framework, the acquisition organization may have enduring responsibilities for providing on-call technical expertise to help resolve escalated operational issues.

In addition to operating and maintaining the COTS/GOTS product and service, the execution of technical refresh/modernization strategies and other follow-on activities takes place in this phase. Analysis of subsequent requirements across the DISA portfolios should be conducted to ensure that efforts are not duplicated and the best approach is identified. If a refresh or follow-on activity is not required, the phase concludes with a decision for project disposal.

For more information on Operations and Support, reference Chapter IV, Section 12.

5 Integrated COTS/GOTS (Model 5)

The integrated COTS/GOTS model (see Figure 10) is used when the focus is primarily on the integration of two or more COTS/GOTS products that are integrated into an existing system. New software development is minimized. This model includes IT Environment acquisitions (e.g. Infrastructure as a Service (IaaS) and Platform as a Service (PaaS)). DISA is responsible for overall systems integration. The acquisition of integrated COTS/GOTS for an enterprise service should refer to Model 6.

Some of the key characteristics of this acquisition model include:

- Developing a configuration and change management strategy.
- Strategy to address implementation and maintenance based on the frequency of vendor/contractor release cycles.
- Assessing current interface standards and interface technology for the development of the interface requirements and design.
- Strategy for incorporating newer versions of technologies.
- Identifying of the data rights on the target system to facilitate integration.

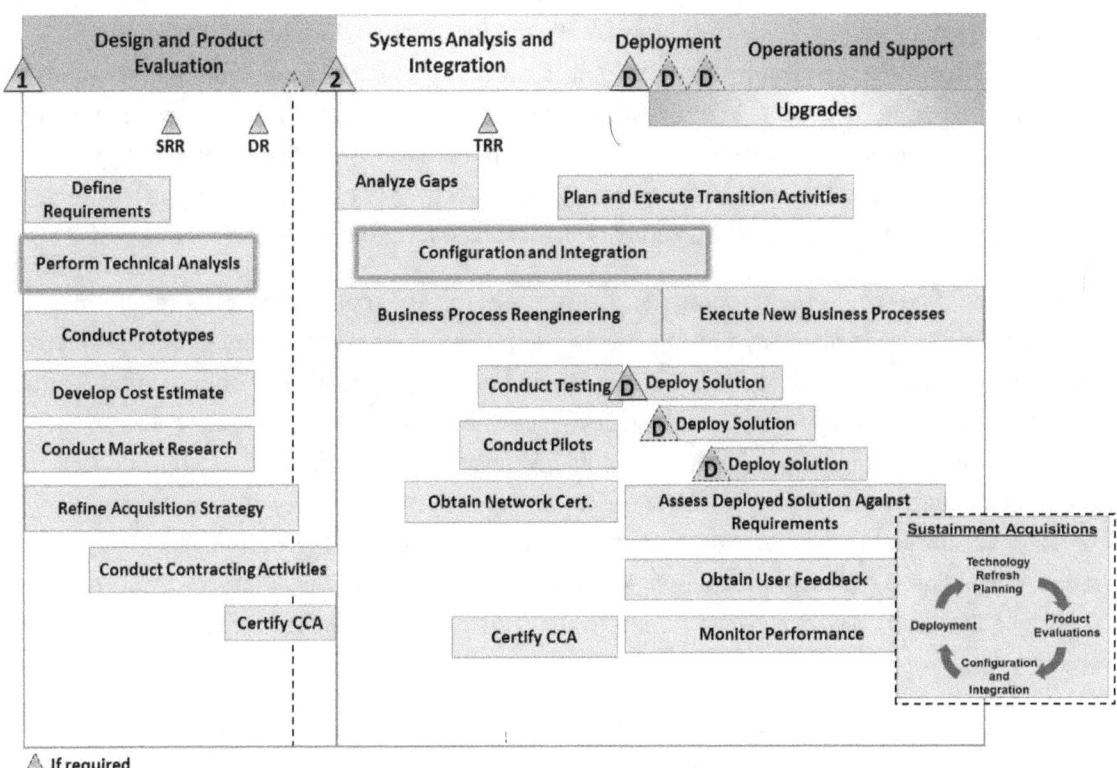

Figure 10 Integrated COTS/GOTS Model Process View

61

5.1 Design and Product Evaluation Phase

Activities to be performed in this phase continue building on the documents and decisions from the initiation phase. The requirements are refined and finalized in this phase using the analyses of alternatives from the initiation phase. The activities in this phase—shaping requirements, defining the technical baseline, and conducting technical analysis of COTS/GOTS, cost estimates, market research, contracting, etc. —are performed in parallel and tightly aligned. All of the processes influence each other and will help the acquisition team develop the optimal strategy for the acquisition.

The following activities, documents, and plans must be executed, developed, and completed/approved.

5.1.1 Define Requirements

In concert with the analysis and strategies in this phase, the acquisition team will refine and finalize the requirements to effectively baseline and acquire the capabilities.

All members of the acquisition team should be strongly engaged in the requirements definition process, especially the requirements (user) community. Defining requirements begins with the drafting of a statement of the user's need, including the level of performance and availability the end-user would like to have. This statement should define the operational need for the item, including the intended use, and should also define the desired support services, such as training, testing, maintenance, and repair services. Stating requirements in terms of objectives, rather than specifying exactly how the item should be manufactured or the service performed, allows for a greater flexibility in determining the appropriate solution. Stating the requirements in terms of objectives will also facilitate the development of a Statement of Objectives/Performance Work Statement in the contracting phase.

As the process to refine requirements continues, logistics support that could impact the requirements should also be considered. The ability to pro-actively monitor service delivery to the end-user, and to promptly identify and recover from service outages, should be considered in developing requirements if appropriate. Additionally, factors such as product availability and upgrade plans, as well as customary warranty and reliability assurances, should be considered and their impact appropriately discussed in the acquisition strategy. The clear definition of hardware and software interfaces is another factor to consider in developing requirements and acquisition strategies when several subsystems will be linked together within a single system. Periodically, software interfaces may need to be redesigned to keep up with evolving commercial technology and improve total system performance.

The requirements should be captured in a Capability Requirements Document. For additional information on how to requirements, reference Chapter IV, Section 1.

Key Questions:
- Who is the customer base for the requirement?
- How is the customer involved in the ongoing requirements documentation and prioritization process?

- Is the requirement defined in terms of end-user experience?
- Has the operations community been engaged in informing the requirements?
- Does the program have a process to regularly update, refine, and reprioritize requirements?
- Are a broad range of end users that can be actively engaged to evaluate prototypes and support source selection activities to achieve service buy-in?

5.1.2 Perform Technical Analysis

A comprehensive technical analysis is probably one of the most important aspects of this acquisition model. This requires extensive analysis of existing COTS and GOTS products, the technical environment they must operate in, and their ability to meet the user requirements to accomplish their mission objectives. This is a dynamic set of tradeoffs between the three elements.

The team should begin with an initial set of requirements to meet the mission objectives to provide an initial scope. These requirements and scope will likely adjust based on the technical analysis. Often the users' interest in an existing COTS/GOTS product may be the initial driver for the acquisition.

The team will identify, benchmark, and analyze viable COTS/GOTS products using the results of market research. This includes first-hand analysis from systems engineering, information assurance, and users' perspectives. The team can also leverage any independent analysis of commercial products conducted by industry experts. A side-by-side comparison of key features, costs, risks, IA, usability, integration, scalability, and related factors should be compiled. During the analysis, some products may be deemed non-viable by not meeting basic standards. The team can focus their analysis on the remaining ones, essentially down-selecting along the way to a suitable number to select from. Options may include different combinations of COTS/GOTS products. .

The technical analysis should investigate the design, security, integration, support, performance and other elements of the GOTS software. Software Questionnaires are available containing over 50 questions for program teams to consider for COTS, GOTS, Open Source Software, Custom Software, and Hosted Applications. Contact the Acquisition Support Center for a copy of the questionnaires.

The technical environment must be clearly understood. It should comply with DISA's Enterprise Architectures, and the team should actively collaborate with the Chief Engineers Panel (CEP) and other architecture owners (e.g., DISA EE3). The acquisition strategy should clearly identify points in the process where the program will consult with the CEP. Each viable product should be assessed as to how it would fit and operate within the architecture. DISA (or another DoD organization) may have already certified some products for Information Assurance. Reciprocity should be leveraged to the maximum extent to avoid duplicative and lengthy certifications.

The program team must determine how the proposed acquisition will fit into the DoD information network (DoDIN) architecture and what existing commercial, federal, or DoD standards exist that require interfaces to the infrastructure for other existing services. The standards and architectural

63

requirements will help the team in conducting prototyping activities and market research and in developing cost estimates.

5.1.2.1 Develop a Technical Baseline

The technical baseline manages and tracks the evolution of requirements, designs, configurations, development, integration, test, and other elements. It should serve as the foundation for the other programmatic elements (acquisition strategy, cost, test, etc.). As the program progresses through the acquisition lifecycle, the technical baseline will mature with increasing rigor, number of data sources, and fidelity of details.

For additional information on technical baselines, reference Chapter IV, Section 2.1.

Key Questions:
- Is there a comprehensive, complete, current, and independently verified technical baseline aligned to the cost baseline, requirements, budgets, schedules, and enterprise architectures?
- Is the program leveraging existing hardware platforms and enterprise architectures, standards, and interfaces?
- Does the design integrate mature technologies and align to DISA architectures, standards, and interfaces?
- Does the design anticipate technological evolution?
- Does the design consider Mission Assurance?
- Have current interface standards and interface technology been assessed and factored into the development of the interface requirements and the feasible design?

5.1.3 Conduct Prototypes

The acquisition team should conduct piloting/prototyping activities as needed for risk reduction activities. The program team can begin prototyping activities armed with a thorough understanding of requirements, standards, and market offerings. This step is appropriate if there is significant doubt or risk that commercial offerings or existing capabilities can be integrated to meet the established requirements. If the risk is upheld by the prototyping activities and market research, the program team may want to consider changing the acquisition strategy toward a development approach. More commonly, however, these activities will help the program team refine the acquisition strategy and shape the contracting activities.

For additional information on prototypes, reference Chapter IV, Section 9.

Key Questions:
- Are a broad range of users actively engaged to evaluate prototypes to achieve service buy-in?

5.1.4 Develop Cost Estimate

The cost estimate for an Integrated COTS acquisition may involve costs to license the existing software, costs to configure according to requirements, costs to adapt the products to the DoD Information Network (DODIN), and recurring costs to host the capability in the Defense Enterprise Computing

Centers (DECCs). The preference for this COTS-based model is based on the expectation that these costs should be significantly lower than those expected of a developmental approach.

The acquisition team should request cost support from the Chief Financial Executive (CFE) support team. The resulting cost estimate must be compared against the available budget to determine affordability. The acquisition team lead is required to regularly identify means to reduce program costs throughout the program lifecycle to deliver the best value to the Defense enterprise.

Once the acquisition team identifies that suitable commercial products or services are available in the marketplace to meet the government's need, the government should use commercially available pricing information for the cost estimate. An important aspect of the cost estimate is the consideration of lifecycle costs, including configuration control and logistics support. The degrees of contractor configuration control and logistics support should relate to total cost, performance, and risk. This is critical because the government does not control how the vendor schedules and manages releases/versions, that could adversely impact the systems with which it interfaces. The management structure, including the costs of managing change (both the design aspects as well as potentially supporting multiple configurations), must be considered.

The use of commercial products or components also requires lifecycle planning for change, and this should be incorporated in the cost estimate. Carefully consider the possibility, and associated costs, of any custom integration software that may be required to ensure legacy programs will operate with and on any new hardware and software upgrades. For example, when the vendor updates their operating system, which the government has elected to use, not all programs procured through a different vendor may be necessarily operating on a plug-and-play basis. Integration or "glue" code may need to be developed and maintained. The cost estimate must also include any annual licensing fees for COTS software. Technology refresh and/or upgrades and the associated intervals should be considered and included. It must include planning for technology refreshment and maintaining any associated software after production. This includes how changes (for obsolescence/ technology refreshment and maintaining the software) will be budgeted and executed along with the necessary technical data required to sustain the system throughout the lifecycle.

For additional information on cost estimates, reference Chapter IV, Section 4.

Key Questions:
- Has a sufficient technical/cost tradeoff analysis been conducted?
- Are licensing models (per user, per processor, per concurrent user, etc.) analyzed and understood for COTS products?
- Is life-cycle support and cost sharing required for GOTS products?
- Does the cost estimate include configuration control and logistics support needs?
- Have technology refresh and upgrades been factored into the cost estimate?
- Have post-deployment operational costs over the full lifecycle been included in cost estimates?

5.1.5 Conduct Market Research / Industry Engagement

The acquisition team should continue with the market research that was conducted in the initiation phase. Market research feeds prototyping activities, cost estimates, acquisition strategy refinement, and contracting activities.

Product evaluation is a critical element of this phase and active industry engagement can be an invaluable part of the process. Through market research and industry engagement, the acquisition team should have a list of potential COTS/GOTS solutions. Information about GOTS products can be obtained from Government sources such as the Program of Record, user community, development community, etc., This candidate list will often offer a wide variety of features, capabilities, risks, and opportunities. The evaluation of candidate products will help determine the feasibility of the final requirements and scope of the program or project. As the acquisition team performs the technical analysis, they should actively engage industry to identify and understand COTS product features, ratings, costs, risks, and more. Collaborating with independent experts who review these products is another valuable source of information to product selection. Industry engagement must be done in accordance with contracting officer guidance.

The acquisition team is also encouraged to use a Request for Information (RFI) or use an industry day to understand the breadth and depth of capabilities available in the marketplace to fulfill the government needs. The acquisition team can also use vendor demonstrations and product information to support the requirements.

The acquisition team should also look at open source products to adapt and deliver for DISA needs. Open source is a cost effective alternative to COTS/GOTS, and could come from commercial communities (e.g., Apache) or government communities (e.g., GOSS).

A summary of the market research that was conducted for the acquisition should be included in the acquisition strategy and any relevant acquisition plan.

For additional information on market research, reference Chapter IV, Section 6.2.

5.1.6 Refine Acquisition Strategy

This activity should build on acquisition strategy developed in the initiation phase and the analysis from this planning and strategic analysis phase. The following factors should be considered in the acquisition strategy:

- Supplier capabilities
- Logistics support
- Product availability
- Technology refreshment (including upgrades, modernization, technology insertion strategies)
- Customary warranty
- Reliability assurances

66

- Data rights
- Hardware and software interfaces

A technology refreshment strategy ensures systems stay current with the latest commercial technology and when appropriately planned, eliminates or at least reduces total system upgrades. Technology refreshment should be planned and designed into the system early in its life cycle because it will require an Open Systems Architecture design, or commercial standards-based architecture, to maximize COTS "plug and play" refreshments. In addition, the strategy should address how long the vendor plans to maintain older software versions as part of the lifecycle sustainment plan. A strategy for deployment should also be included that addresses transition, data migration, data cleansing, and data conversion.

For additional information on acquisition strategy, reference Chapter IV, Section 3.

Key Questions:
- Is there a capacity/scalability management strategy and plan?
- What is the strategy for incorporating newer versions of technologies?
- How long will the vendor support and maintain older software versions?
- What is the approach for providing a tiered-level of technical customer support?
- What is the deployment plan to get to the target solution?
- Is the product/service a candidate for a DISA standard processing environment (e.g., RACE, FORGE.mil)?
- Are the resources requirements for the DISA standard processing environment and the associated migration activities adequately addressed in the acquisition strategy?
- If the service is not a candidate for the standard processing environment, has a waiver been obtained?
- Does the strategy plan specify the use of DISA standardized Service Operations tools (e.g. for pro-active monitoring, service-level compliance, and trouble-ticketing)?
- Does the strategy plan specify the operations functions that will support the capability (e.g. cognizant Service Desk, Technical Management, IT Operations Management, and Access Management teams) and how they will be resourced?
- Does the program have sufficient systems engineering processes, reviews?
- Is there a change management process for design and requirements changes?

5.1.7 Conduct Contracting Activities

The contracting requirements for an integrated COTS/GOTS acquisition can vary greatly. In some cases, the acquisition team can acquire COTS/GOTS hardware and software products, as well as any necessary integration support, in a single combined contract. In other cases, it may be in the best interest of the government to contract for these items under separate arrangements. The acquisition team should look at different combinations of contracting arrangements to determine the best strategy for the

acquisition. The level of integration complexity, the ability of the government to manage and maintain a variety of COTS/GOTS hardware and software products, and pass-through and overhead costs are all factors that should be considered in this analysis. The results of this analysis as well as the overall contracting strategy should be documented in the acquisition strategy.

When contracting for integrated COTS/GOTS, the acquisition team should take the following points into consideration:

- The source selection strategy should be based on best value, and the evaluation of the offerors' SLAs should be an important evaluation criterion.
- List all additional and optional fees in the contract, such as additional storage fees and custom reports.
- The contract should clearly identify who owns any customizations or enhancements, especially if the government pays for them as a "work product" developed solely for government-use.
- The government should clearly identify rights to COTS licensing and service data to enable transition to follow-on services and competition of sustainment or enhancement efforts.
- Include language that states who owns data during all of its lifecycle, including when data is transferred or exchanged (data in transit) and during storage (data at rest).
- Include language regarding who bears the risk for loss of data in transit.
- Define what the contractor's responsibilities are in the event of 1) a security breach (e.g., ensure they provide an immediate notice if data may be compromised); 2) an outage; and 3) termination (e.g., ensure the provider will cooperate with the return of government data in a format and manner previously agreed, and with no additional fees for the return of data). Operational stakeholders should be consulted to ensure that contractor operational actions are integrated with the DISA Service Operations Framework, and that service operational status is appropriately up-channeled to DISA.
- Include confidentiality language relative to the DoD and the Federal Information Security Management Act (FISMA).
- Obtain detailed information about the service provider's security processes and procedures, including data flow diagrams.
- Ensure that the DoD is involved in reviewing and determining what data the provider will store and what layers of security need to be in place. This includes making sure all applicable Information Assurance (IA) Policy and regulatory documentation is made part of the agreement reference list.
- Confirm how data access will be limited, including review of the different user permission roles offered, the various accessibility parameters for each role, and the administrator's access rights (e.g., ensure all users' actions can be tracked).
- Include language confirming the contractor's business continuity plan, specifying redundancy requirements to include, at a minimum, data backup and recovery methods/infrastructure/

processes. Also, have the contractor certify that they will participate with the government in disaster recovery testing at specific time intervals (e.g., once every two years) without charge.

- Clearly identify the customary warranties available for the COTS product or service.
- Include associate contractor agreement clauses for acquisitions that require the contractor to work with another DISA contractor.
- Include a transition CLIN for both transition-in as well as transition-out at the end of the contract period.

For additional information on contracting, reference Chapter IV, Section 6.

Key Questions:
- Does the contract strategy support appropriate competition across the commercial marketplace for specific technologies and integration and support activities?
- Will the contracting strategy enable the program team to transition the service to a replacement capability or a new competition for contractor support?

5.1.8 Certify Clinger-Cohen Act

Clinger-Cohen Act (CCA) compliance by DISA CIO is required. For additional information on CCA compliance and certification, reference Chapter IV, Section 8.

5.2 Decision Point 2

At Decision Point 2, the Decision Authority reviews analyses and strategies to develop the capabilities, ensures that the design integrates mature technologies aligned to enterprise architectures, and verifies that program affordability to meet validated requirements within the available budget. The Decision Authority approves the release of the RFP or contract award at Decision Point 2.

In addition to the key questions identified above, the acquisition team should be prepared to answer the following standard questions at Decision Point 2:

Standard Questions for Decision Point 2:
- Are the program requirements validated and prioritized?
- Have rigorous cost estimates been conducted?
- Is the program affordable within the available budget?
- Does the contract strategy address risk, incentives, data rights, and competition across the lifecycle?
- Does the team actively engage industry to shape strategy?
- Is test integrated and scaled based on program risk?
- Is there a transition plan to deploy capabilities?
- Is there a plan to operate the capability in accordance with the DISA Service Operations Framework?
- Is there a realistic Integrated Master Schedule?
- Has the program identified and mitigated risks?

- Does the strategy satisfy the customer's requirements?
- Is the strategy designed to maximize competition?
- How will the contract type minimize risk to the government?
- Are there existing contract vehicles available for the required services? If not, should DISA develop an enterprise contract vehicle for this service?
- Does the strategy appropriately leverage contract type and objective incentives to motivate contractors to exceed minimum performance requirements?
- Have conflict-of-interest issues been addressed and eliminated or mitigation plans established?

The following information is also required for Decision Point 2 approval:

Information Required at Decision Point 2:
- Acquisition Strategy (includes Technical Analysis, Market Research, Pilot/Prototype Results, Information Support Plan, Technical Data Rights Strategy, Systems Engineering Plan, Architecture Strategy, Test and Evaluation Management Plan, and Lifecycle Sustainment Plan)
- Capability Requirements Document
- Concept of Operations
- Services Operations Annex
- Acquisition Program Baseline
- Cost Estimate
- Acquisition Plan
- Request for Proposal and Other Contracting Docs
- Service Level Agreements (when applicable)
- Business Processes Reengineering (when applicable)
- Clinger-Cohen Act Compliance

The acquisition team will prepare an Acquisition Decision Memorandum (ADM) and the Decision Authority will sign it. The ADM will capture the key decisions in the meeting, any action items for the acquisition team, and any guidance or deviations from policy and guidance for criteria for the next acquisition phase and deployment decision.

5.3 Systems Analysis and Integration Phase

Activities to be performed in this phase include configuring and integrating the COTS/GOTS products, integrated testing, and obtaining network certification approval.

5.3.1 Analyze Gaps

While the team conducted a technical analysis in the previous phase, a gap assessment is needed once the COTS/GOTS products have been acquired. The acquisition team, in collaboration with the contractor and end user, should determine if any gaps exist between the intended functionality of the COTS/GOTS capability and the program needs. If gaps are identified, the acquisition team should consider a variety of options to include alternative technical solutions, business process reengineering,

70

and product customization. Once gaps have been identified, assessed, and solutions explored, stakeholders and decision makers can determine the way ahead based on risk, budgets, schedule, and other factors. The proposed technical solution must be vetted by the DISA Chief Engineers Panel (CEP) prior to acquisition.

5.3.2 Configuration and Integration

COTS and GOTS products will often require extensive configuration and integration with related systems, platforms, and infrastructure. The details of this should have been captured in the acquisition strategy and related program documents prior to Decision Point 2 as well as in the RFP and contract(s). DISA staff and contractors will often have shared responsibility for configuration and integration of IT capabilities for an enterprise service. DISA staff with knowledge of enterprise architectures, platforms, standards, interfaces, and mission assurance responsibilities will always be ultimately responsible. Contractors who either developed the COTS/GOTS software or provide support services will likely have the knowledge of the software details for configuration.

Roles and responsibilities must be clearly defined across all stakeholders to ensure a common understanding. The more complex or risky programs may require a more comprehensive approach to include identification and resolution of issues and consideration of likely IT environments. Teams may use collaboration software, recurring meetings, and other methods to ensure all stakeholders are aware of the status, issues, and resolutions.

In some cases, the program / vendor team will acquire the selected COTS/GOTS components, configure, and integrate them into a pilot service to demonstrate capabilities to customer representatives. These efforts are analogous to development activities and warrant close working relationships between the program office, vendor, and customer representatives to ensure the efforts do not stray from established requirements and expectations.

5.3.3 Business Process Reengineering

Business Process Reengineering (BPR) is redesigning the way work is done to better support the organization's mission and reduce costs. The intent of BPR in this model is to redesign DISA business processes, to the maximum extent possible, to conform to the best practice business rules adopted by industry. In most cases, it is best to adopt the COTS/GOTS solution "out-of-the-box" rather than adapting the product to accommodate existing systems and processes.

For COTS acquisitions, additional BPR is conducted after program initiation, to reengineer an organization's retained processes to match available COTS processes.

For additional information on BPR activities, reference Chapter IV, Section 5.

5.3.4 Conduct Testing

After completing integration and configuration activities, the government must conduct acceptance and operational testing of the service prior to a formal deployment decision. PEO test engineers, JITC

testers, and operational user representatives will assess the service according to their roles and provide input to the deployment decision.

For additional information on testing activities, reference Chapter IV, Section 10.

5.3.5 Conduct Pilots

The acquisition team should conduct piloting/prototyping activities as needed for risk reduction activities.

For additional information on pilots, reference Chapter IV, Section 9.

5.3.6 Obtain Network Certification

Validation of the adapted COTS/GOTS products using an approved test plan is required to obtain network certification and add the products to the Service Catalog. A network certification is obtained through a knowledge point review and documented in a decision memorandum approved by the DA.

During configuration and integration, the service must also undergo certification and accreditation. This process may be simplified if the components of the solution are already accredited within the DoD Information Networks. Prior to piloting, the COTS/GOTS product must have at least an Interim Authority to Operate (IATO) to allow customers or end users to test and review the product. Once the pilot process and testing efforts are complete, the program/project should obtain a full Authority to Operate (ATO) prior to deployment.

5.3.7 Certify Clinger-Cohen Act

Clinger-Cohen Act (CCA) compliance by DISA CIO is required. For additional information on CCA compliance and certification, reference Chapter IV Section 8.

5.4 Deployment Decision(s)

Deployment Decisions(s) by the Decision Authority will review the testing and certification reports to verify that the program meets performance requirements, validate that the capabilities meet the operational sponsor/ enterprise's needs, and ensure that there is a sound strategy to operate, maintain, support, and evolve the capability.

The acquisition team should be prepared to answer the following standard questions at Deployment Decision:

Standard Questions for Deployment Decisions:
• Has sufficient testing been conducted on the program?
• Do test results show the program has been implemented based on requirements/customer needs?
• Has the program been independently validated and verified?
• Has the program completed the required elements of the integrated checklist?
• Does the program have a suitable plan to operate and sustain the capabilities with appropriate IA?

- Does the program have a suitable plan to provide patches, upgrades, and additional releases?
- Does the program have sufficient budget to meet estimated operational and sustainment costs?
- Does the organization responsible for operating the capability concur with deployment?
- Do the appropriate stakeholders agree the capability is ready to be deployed?

In addition, the following information is required for Deployment Decision approval:

Information Required at Deployment Decision(s):
- Updated Acquisition Strategy (includes Lifecycle Sustainment Plan, Information Assurance Strategy, Technical Data Rights Strategy, Information Support Plan, Item Unique Identifier Plan, Performance Management Strategy, Transition to DECC, and Support Posture)
- Operational Test and Evaluation Results
- Updated Services Operations Annex
- Integrated Checklist
- JITC Certification
- Clinger-Cohen Act Compliance
- Acquisition Lessons Learned and Best Practices
- Authorization to Operate (ATO)

5.5 Operations and Support Phase

The objectives of the operations and support phase are to operate and support the capability through the end of the intended lifecycle. Additional releases and considerations for follow-on and/or subsequent technical refresh acquisitions are evaluated in this phase.

During the Operations and Support phase, the capability will be operated using the operational processes defined in the Defense Enterprise Service Management Framework. Depending on the agreed operational concept documented as part of the Service Operations Framework, the acquisition organization may have enduring responsibilities for providing on-call technical expertise to help resolve escalated operational issues.

In addition to operating the program/project, acquisition planning for technical refresh, modernization, and/or follow-on activities begins in this phase. Analysis of subsequent requirements across the DISA portfolios should be conducted to ensure that efforts are not duplicated and the best approach is identified. If a refresh or follow-on activity is not required, the phase concludes with a decision for project disposal.

For more information on Operations and Support, reference Chapter IV, Section 12.

6 Enterprise Services (Model 6)

An Enterprise Service is a capability that DISA has developed and delivered to the DoD enterprise via the DISA Service Catalog. Enterprise users can learn about a service and gain access to it via the DISA Customer Management Executives (CMEs) or the DISA Service Catalog. The services are categorized as enterprise application services and enterprise infrastructure services. Application services (e.g., DoD Enterprise Email (DEE) and Defense Connect Online (DCO)) are sometimes referred to as user-facing services, since they are directly accessible by users. Likewise, infrastructure services (e.g., Enterprise Messaging (EM) and Enterprise Service Management (ESM)) are sometimes referred to as machine-facing services, since they are generally accessed by other applications. Most enterprise services are acquired as an integration and configuration of COTS/GOTS products; however, an enterprise service can be acquired via any of the acquisition models (e.g., custom development or managed IT service). The model framework depicted in Figure 11 is based on an integrated COTS/GOTS acquisition, but it should be tailored as appropriate if using a development or services acquisition strategy.

Some of the key characteristics of this acquisition model include:

- Identifying the customer base for the acquisition and developing a process to obtain continuous customer involvement in the ongoing requirements documentation and prioritization process.
- Establishing a business model for a cost and pricing strategy to recover investment costs as well as the ongoing O&M costs.
- Developing a customer relationship management (CRM) strategy that is incorporated into the acquisition strategy and deployment plan.
- Developing a strategy for capacity/scalability management and incorporating newer versions of technologies.
- Developing an approach for providing a tiered-level of technical customer support.

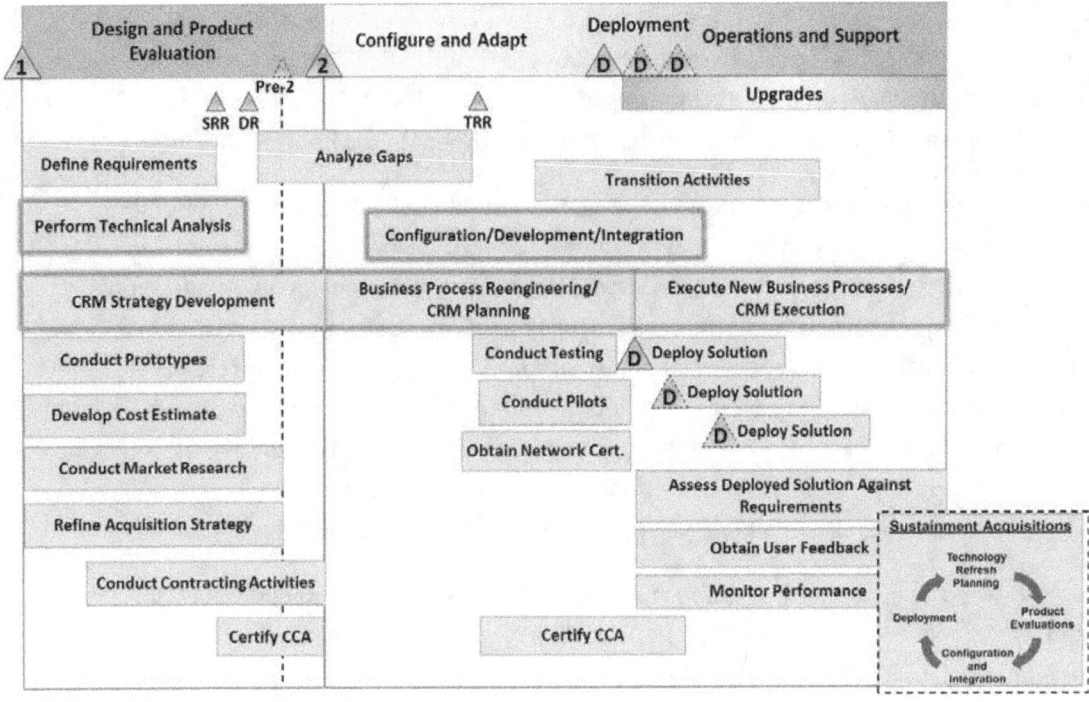

Figure 11 Enterprise Services Model Process View

6.1 Design and Product Evaluation Phase

Activities to be performed in this phase continue building on the documents and decisions from the initiation phase. The requirements are refined and finalized in this phase using the analyses of alternatives from the initiation phase. The activities in this phase—shaping requirements, defining the technical baseline, and conducting technical analysis of COTS/GOTS, cost estimates, market research, contracting, etc.—are performed in parallel and tightly aligned. All of the processes influence each other and will help the acquisition team develop the optimal strategy for the acquisition. The results of the following activities feed into one another to complete the program team's understanding of the need and refinement of the strategy for acquiring the planned enterprise service.

The following activities, documents, and plans must be executed, developed, and completed/approved

6.1.1 Define Requirements

In concert with the analysis and strategies in this phase, the acquisition team will refine and finalize the requirements to effectively baseline and acquire the capabilities.

All members of the acquisition team should be strongly engaged in the requirements definition process, especially the requirements (user) community. Defining requirements begins with the drafting of a statement of the user's need, including the level of performance and availability the end-user would like to have. This statement should define the operational need for the item, including the intended use, and should also define the desired support services, such as training, testing, maintenance, and

75

repair services. Stating requirements in terms of objectives, rather than specifying exactly how the item should be manufactured or the service performed, allows for greater flexibility in determining the appropriate solution. Stating the requirements in terms of objectives will also facilitate the development of a Statement of Objectives/Performance Work Statement in the contracting phase.

As the process to refine requirements continues, logistics support that could impact the requirements should also be considered. The ability to pro-actively monitor service delivery to the end-user, and to promptly identify and recover from service outages, should be considered in developing requirements if appropriate. Additionally, factors such as product availability and upgrade plans, as well as customary warranty and reliability assurances, should be considered and their impact appropriately discussed in the acquisition planning stage. The clear definition of hardware and software interfaces is another factor to consider in developing requirements and acquisition strategies when several subsystems will be linked within a single system. Periodically, software interfaces may need to be redesigned to keep up with evolving commercial technology and improve total system performance.

For an enterprise service, the customer base needs to be identified and continuously engaged. It is critical to capture their functional requirements, prioritize them within and across user groups, discuss and demonstrate potential COTS/GOTS solutions, and understand the cost/performance tradeoffs. Any operational support required for implementation, training, help desk, etc., should also be captured and vetted. In this model, the capabilities of existing COTS/GOTS products are the primary driver of the program's functionality to meet the operational mission. An additional challenge for an enterprise service acquisition is the management of potentially competing priorities among customers across the DoD.

The requirements should be captured in a Capability Requirements Document. For additional information on requirements, reference Chapter IV, Section 1.

> **Key Questions:**
> - Who is the customer base for the requirement?
> - How is the customer involved in the ongoing requirements documentation and prioritization process?
> - Is the requirement defined in terms of end-user experience?
> - Has the operations community been engaged in informing the requirements?
> - Does the program have a process to regularly update, refine, and reprioritize requirements?
> - Are a broad range of users actively engaged to evaluate prototypes and support source selection activities to achieve service buy-in?

6.1.2 Perform Technical Analysis

A comprehensive technical analysis is probably one of the most important aspects of this acquisition model. This requires extensive analysis of existing COTS and GOTS products, the technical environment they must operate in, and their ability to meet the user requirements to accomplish their mission objectives. This is a dynamic set of tradeoffs between the three elements.

The team should begin with an initial set of requirements to meet the mission objectives to provide an initial scope. These requirements and scope will likely adjust based on the technical analysis. Often the users' interest in an existing COTS/GOTS product may be the initial driver for the acquisition.

The team will identify, benchmark, and analyze viable COTS/GOTS products for consideration in the Enterprise Service using the results of market research. This includes first-hand analysis from systems engineering, information assurance, and users' perspectives. The team can also leverage any independent analysis of commercial products conducted by industry experts. A side-by-side comparison of key features, costs, risks, IA, usability, integration, scalability, and related factors should be compiled. During the analysis, some products may be deemed non-viable by not meeting basic standards. The team can focus their analysis on the remaining ones, essentially down-selecting along the way to a suitable number to select from. Enterprise Services options may include different combinations of COTS/GOTS products.

The technical analysis should investigate the design, security, integration, support, performance and other elements of the GOTS software. Software Questionnaires containing over 50 questions for program teams to consider for COTS, GOTS, Open Source Software, Custom Software, and Hosted Applications. Contact the CAE for a copy of the questionnaires.

The technical environment must be clearly understood. It should comply with DISA's Enterprise Architectures and the team should actively collaborate with the Chief Engineers Panel (CEP) and other architecture owners (e.g., DISA EE3). The acquisition plan should clearly identify points in the process where the program will consult with the CEP. Each viable product should be assessed as to how it would fit and operate within the architecture. DISA (or another DoD organization) may have already certified some products for Information Assurance. Reciprocity should be leveraged to the maximum extent to avoid duplicative and lengthy certifications.

The program team must determine how the proposed acquisition will fit into the DoD information network (DoDIN) architecture and what existing commercial, federal, or DoD standards exist that specify required interfaces to infrastructure other existing services. The standards and architectural requirements will aid the team in conducting prototyping activities, market research, and developing cost estimates.

6.1.2.1 Develop a Technical Baseline

The technical baseline manages and tracks the evolution of requirements, designs, configurations, development, integration, test, and other elements. It should serve as the foundation for the other programmatic elements (acquisition strategy, cost, test, etc.). As the program progresses through the acquisition lifecycle, the technical baseline will mature with increasing rigor, number of data sources, and fidelity of details.

For additional information on technical baselines, reference Chapter IV, Section 2.1.

Key Questions:

- Is there a comprehensive, complete, current, and independently verified technical baseline aligned to the cost baseline, requirements, budgets, schedules, and enterprise architectures?
- Is the program leveraging existing hardware platforms and enterprise architectures, standards, and interfaces?
- Does the design integrate mature technologies and align to DISA architectures, standards, and interfaces?
- Does the design anticipate technological evolution?
- Does the design consider Mission Assurance (i.e. how security and service delivery will be managed)?
- Have current interface standards and interface technology been assessed and factored into the development of the interface requirements and the feasible design?

6.1.3 Customer Relationship Management (CRM) Strategy

DISA is increasingly delivering services to the full DoD enterprise. This requires active collaboration with warfighters, CIOs, and other stakeholders to fully understand the mission need, CONOPS, requirements, priorities, tradeoffs, and operational environment. DISA cannot operate in a vacuum to design, acquire/develop, and deliver capabilities. The scope of the program/project, individual releases, technical performance, and many other factors need to be collaboratively developed with all key stakeholders from the earliest phases and throughout the program's lifecycle. This is a complex and challenging task for the acquisition team, but it is critical to program success.

Development of a CRM strategy early in the acquisition process is an especially important activity. Consideration for how the program will manage CRM, to include user identification, requirements gathering, SLAs, and help desk services, should take place as early as the initiation phase for the acquisition to ensure that the necessary resources and processes are in place for proper CRM execution. An enterprise service may be proposed in recognition of a new unfulfilled DoD need or the promotion of an existing service for use across the DoD, or with the goal of consolidating multiple existing services. Each case presents different challenges regarding managing the relationship with stakeholders and governance associated with service requirements. Unlike establishing a capability for a single customer, the program team will likely coordinate with stakeholders from the Joint Staff, DoD CIO office, and representatives of the community of interest from combatant commands, military services, and DoD agencies.

The CRM strategy should continue to be matured throughout the program's lifecycle. Empowered representatives must be identified commensurate with the user size, location, program complexity, risk, and other factors. There may be a small board of officials/reps to drive requirements, convey CONOPS, collaborate with acquisition teams, provide feedback on pilot/prototype capabilities, and manage cost, schedule, and performance tradeoffs. Ideally a representative set of end users is available for piloting, prototyping, demonstrating, operational assessments, operational test, and related activities from across the enterprise. The CRM strategy should identify these groups and individuals, along with the methods and frequencies to engage them. Some relationships require

personal one-on-one collaboration from a program manager, chief engineer, or PEO. Others may be a monthly or quarterly meeting of a small group of individuals. Virtual meetings, forums, and demonstrations can be effective to collaborate with warfighters across the DoD.

Service Level Agreements (SLAs) are necessary to establish performance thresholds for the service and to ensure quality of service, interoperability, and availability of network management data exchanged between systems and with any authorized user IAW the DODI Network Management policy. Operational performance of the services defined in the SLA will be monitored, measured, and reported against the commitments defined in the agreement.

For additional information on SLAs, reference Chapter IV, Section 7.

Key Questions:
- Has a customer relationship management (CRM) strategy been incorporated into the acquisition strategy and deployment plan?
- Have appropriate CRM processes been identified and established?
- Have SLAs been established to manage customer relationships?
- Is an existing user community or governance structure associated with the proposed enterprise service?
- How will competing priorities be adjudicated among diverse stakeholders?

6.1.4 Conduct Prototypes

The acquisition team should conduct piloting/prototyping activities as needed for risk reduction activities. The program team can begin prototyping activities armed with a thorough understanding of requirements, standards, and market offerings. This step is appropriate if there is significant doubt or risk that commercial offerings or existing capabilities can be integrated to meet the established requirements. If the risk is upheld by the prototyping activities and market research, the program team may want to consider changing the acquisition strategy toward a development approach. More commonly, however, these activities will help the program team refine the acquisition strategy and shape the contracting activities.

For additional information on prototypes, reference Chapter IV, Section 9.

Key Question:
- Are a broad range of users actively engaged to evaluate prototypes and support source selection activities to achieve service buy-in?

6.1.5 Develop Cost Estimate

In the case of an enterprise service that is anticipated to be an integration or configuration of COTS products, the cost estimate may involve costs to license the existing software, costs to configure according to requirements, costs to adapt the products to the DoD Information Network (DODIN), and recurring costs to host the capability in the Defense Enterprise Computing Centers (DECCs). The

preference for this COTS-based model is based on the expectation that these costs should be significantly lower than those expected of a developmental approach.

The acquisition team should request cost support from the Chief Financial Executive (CFE) support team. The resulting cost estimate must be compared against the available budget to determine affordability. Program managers are required to regularly identify means to reduce program costs throughout the program lifecycle to deliver the best value to the defense enterprise.

Once the acquisition team identifies that suitable commercial products or services are available in the marketplace to meet the government's need, the government should use commercially available pricing information for the cost estimate. An important aspect of the cost estimate is the consideration of lifecycle costs, including configuration control and logistics support. The degrees of contractor configuration control and logistics support should relate to total cost, performance, and risk. This is critical because government does not control how the vendor schedules and manages releases/versions, which could adversely impact the systems with which it interfaces. The management structure, including the costs of managing change (both the design aspects as well as potentially supporting multiple configurations), must be considered.

The use of commercial products or components also requires lifecycle planning for change, and this should be incorporated in the cost estimate. Carefully consider the possibility, and associated costs, of any custom integration software that may be required to ensure legacy programs will operate with and on any new hardware and software upgrades. For example, when the vendor updates their operating system, which the government has elected to use, not all programs procured through a different vendor may be necessarily operating on a plug-and-play basis. Integration or "glue" code may need to be developed and maintained. The cost estimate must also include any annual licensing fees for COTS software. Technology refresh and/or upgrades and the associated intervals should be considered and included. It must include planning for technology refreshment and maintaining any associated software after production. This includes how changes (for obsolescence/ technology refreshment and maintaining the software) will be budgeted and executed along with the necessary technical data required to sustain the system throughout the lifecycle.

6.1.5.1   Establish a Business Model

For an enterprise services model, the acquisition team is required to create a cost estimate for the program lifecycle as well as a pricing model that will be used for cost recovery and to charge DoD customers for the use of DISA-provided enterprise services. The development of both a program cost estimate as well as a pricing model is a complex costing endeavor. The acquisition team should work with the CFE office or obtain cost support to perform these activities. The business model must include an assessment of cost recovery strategies on service adoption and usage. The three typical defense working capital fund (DWCF) cost recovery strategies are rate based, subscription based, and direct cost recovery.

A key factor in developing a cost estimate for the enterprise service model is the customer base. An understanding of the level of service required and the price points that are impacted by the number of customers is critical. As the team develops the cost model and estimates, the analysis should drive potential pricing options. Most services have fixed and variable costs to acquire and deliver the capabilities. A minimum customer base should be identified for the acquisition of the capabilities. As the numbers of customers grow, there may be thresholds that drive a significant increase in costs (e.g., additional hardware required). The team must have a comprehensive understanding of the scaling of these costs to effectively develop a pricing strategy. Similarly the pricing model must account for many risks areas, such as risks in cost growth and risks in too many customers, technology refresh cycles, and upgrades.

For additional information on cost estimates, reference Chapter IV, Section 4.

Key Questions:
- How does the cost estimate account for the adjustment of capacity when it needs to be scaled up and down?
- What is the business model for establishing the cost and pricing strategy to recover investment costs as well as the ongoing O&M costs?
- Are licensing models (per user, per processor, per concurrent user, etc.) analyzed and understood for COTS products?
- Is lifecycle support and cost sharing required for GOTS products?
- Does the cost estimate include configuration control and logistics support needs?
- Have technology refresh and upgrades been factored into the cost estimate?
- Has a sufficient technical/cost tradeoff analysis been conducted?
- Have post-deployment operational costs over the full lifecycle been included in cost estimates?

6.1.6 Conduct Market Research / Industry Engagement

The acquisition team should continue with the market research that was conducted in the initiation phase. Market research feeds prototyping activities, cost estimates, acquisition strategy refinement, and contracting activities.

Product evaluation is a critical element of this phase, and active industry engagement can be an invaluable part of the process. Through market research and industry engagement, the acquisition team should have a list of potential COTS/GOTS solutions. Information about GOTS products can be obtained from Government sources such as the Program of Record, user community, development community, etc., This candidate list will often offer a wide variety of features, capabilities, risks, and opportunities. The evaluation of candidate products will help determine the feasibility of the final requirements and scope of the program or project. As the acquisition team performs the technical analysis, they should actively engage industry to identify and understand COTS product features, ratings, costs, risks, and more. Collaborating with independent experts who review these products is

another valuable source of information to product selection. Industry engagement must be done in accordance with contracting officer guidance.

The acquisition team is also encouraged to use a Request for Information (RFI) or use an industry day to understand the breadth and depth of capabilities available in the marketplace to fulfill the government needs. The acquisition team can also use vendor demonstrations and product information to support the requirements.

The acquisition team should also look at open source products to adapt and deliver as an enterprise service. Open source is a cost effective alternative to COTS/GOTS, and could come from commercial communities (e.g., Apache) or government communities (e.g., GOSS).

A summary of the market research that was conducted for the acquisition should be included in the acquisition strategy and any relevant acquisition plan.

For additional information on market research, reference Chapter IV, Section 6.2.

6.1.7 Refine Acquisition Strategy

This activity should build on acquisition strategy developed in the initiation phase and the analysis from this planning and strategic analysis phase. The following factors should be considered in the acquisition strategy development phase:

- Supplier capabilities
- Logistics support
- Product availability
- Upgrade plans
- Customary warranty
- Reliability assurances
- Data rights
- Hardware and software interfaces

For an enterprise services acquisition, the acquisition strategy should address how the acquisition team plans to manage capacity and scalability for the acquisition based on changes to the customer base. The plan should address the anticipated growth of the customer base over the program lifecycle and the impact that it will have on the program in terms of cost and infrastructure capacity. In addition, the strategy should address how the program plans to incorporate newer versions of COTS/GOTS products, and how long the vendor plans to maintain older software versions as part of the lifecycle sustainment plan. A strategy for deployment should also be included to include planning the transition of a large number of users or organizations onto the new system, data migration, data cleansing, and data conversion, and customer relationship management strategy.

All DISA acquisitions will be required to complete a Service Operations Annex, a DISA-unique document developed by the Operations Directorate (OPS) and required by OPS for all new DISA acquisitions. This

is a top-level planning document to help ensure that the acquisition is appropriately integrated into DISA's Service Operations processes and functions. This document includes a service description to ensure that operational support planning is founded on an understanding of what capabilities the service will deliver to end-users. The document requires a summary of the service description, a narrative description of how the service will implement service command & control, and a narrative description of how the service operations processes/functions specified in the DESMF will be implemented (e.g., Event Management, Incident Management, Problem Management, Access Management, Service Desk, IT Operation Management, Technical Management, and Application Management).

For additional information on acquisition strategy, reference Chapter IV, Section 3.

Key Questions:
- Is there a capacity/scalability management strategy and plan?
- What is the strategy for incorporating newer versions of technologies?
- How long will the vendor support and maintain older software versions?
- What is the approach for providing a tiered-level of technical customer support?
- What is the deployment plan to get to the target solution?
- Is the product/service a candidate for a DISA standard processing environment (e.g., RACE, FORGE.mil)?
- Are the resources requirements for the DISA standard processing environment and the associated migration activities adequately addressed in the acquisition strategy?
- If the service is not a candidate for the standard processing environment, has a waiver been obtained?
- Does the strategy plan specify the use of DISA standardized Service Operations tools (e.g. for pro-active monitoring, service-level compliance, and trouble-ticketing)?
- Does the strategy plan specify the operations functions that will support the capability (e.g. cognizant Service Desk, Technical Management, IT Operations Management, and Access Management teams) and how they will be resourced?
- Does the program have sufficient systems engineering processes, reviews?
- Is there a change management process for design and requirements changes?

6.1.8 Conduct Contracting Activities

The contracting, requirements for an enterprise services acquisition can vary greatly. In some cases, the acquisition team can acquire COTS/GOTS hardware and software products, as well as any necessary integration support, in a single combined contract. In other cases, it may be in the best interest of the government to contract for these items under separate arrangements. The acquisition team should look at different combinations of contracting arrangements to determine the best strategy for the acquisition. The level of integration complexity, the ability of the government to manage and maintain a variety a COTS/GOTS hardware and software products, and pass-through and overhead costs are all factors that should be considered in this analysis. The results of the contracting analysis as well as the overall contracting strategy should be documented in the acquisition strategy.

83

When contracting for enterprise service, the acquisition team should make the following considerations;

- The source selection strategy should be based on best value and the evaluation of the offerors' SLAs should be an important evaluation criterion.
- List all additional and optional fees in the contract, such as additional storage fees and custom reports.
- The contract should clearly identify who owns any customizations or enhancements, especially if the government pays for them as a "work product" developed solely for government use.
- The government should clearly identify rights to COTS licensing and service data to enable transition to follow-on services and competition of sustainment or enhancement efforts.
- Include language that states who owns data during all of its lifecycle, including when data is transferred or exchanged (data in transit) and during storage (data at rest).
- Include language regarding who bears the risk for loss of data in transit.
- Define what the contractor's responsibilities are in the event of 1) a security breach (e.g., ensure they provide an immediate notice if data may be compromised); 2) an outage; and 3) termination (e.g., ensure the provider will cooperate with the return of government data in a format and manner previously agreed, and with no additional fees for the return of data). Operational stakeholders should be consulted to ensure that contractor operational actions are integrated with the DISA Service Operations Framework, and that service operational status is appropriately up-channeled to DISA.
- Include confidentiality language relative to the DoD and the Federal Information Security Management Act (FISMA).
- Obtain detailed information about the service provider's security processes and procedures, including data flow diagrams.
- Ensure that the DoD is involved in reviewing and determining what data the provider will store and what layers of security need to be in place. This includes making sure all applicable Information Assurance (IA) Policy and regulatory documentation is made part of the agreement reference list.
- Confirm how data access will be limited, including review of the different user permission roles offered, the various accessibility parameters for each role, and the administrator's access rights (e.g., ensure that all users' actions can be tracked).
- Include language confirming the contractor's business continuity plan, specifying redundancy requirements to include, at a minimum, data backup and recovery methods/infrastructure/ processes. Also, have the contractor certify that they will participate with the government in disaster recovery testing at specific time intervals (e.g., once every two years) without charge.
- Clearly identify the customary warranties available for the COTS product or service.
- Include associate contractor agreement clauses for acquisitions that require the contractor to work with another DISA contractor.

- Include a transition CLIN for both transition-in as well as transition-out at the end of the contract period.
- Enterprise service contracts should define contractor responsibilities to support implementation and deployment activities. Include contract incentives that measure responsiveness to resolving issues during deployment and transition.

For additional information on contracting, reference Chapter IV, Section 6.

Key Questions:
- Has the acquisition team aligned the contract SLAs with the SLAs under the CRM strategy?
- Does the contract strategy support appropriate competition across the commercial marketplace for specific technologies and integration and support activities?
- Will the contracting strategy enable the program team to transition the service to a replacement capability or a new competition for contractor support?

6.1.9 Certify Clinger-Cohen Act

Clinger-Cohen Act (CCA) compliance by DISA CIO is required. For additional information on CCA compliance and certification, reference Chapter IV, Section 8.

6.2 Decision Point 2

At Decision Point 2, the Decision Authority reviews analyses and strategies to develop the capabilities, ensures that the design integrates mature technologies aligned to enterprise architectures, and verifies program affordability to meet validated requirements within the available budget. The Decision Authority approves the release of the RFP or contract/task order award at Decision Point 2.

In addition to the key questions identified above, the acquisition team should be prepared to answer the following standard questions at Decision Point 2:

Standard Questions for Decision Point 2:
- Are the program requirements validated and prioritized?
- Have rigorous cost estimates been conducted?
- Is the program affordable within the available budget?
- Does the contract strategy address risk, incentives, data rights, and competition across the lifecycle?
- Does the team actively engage industry to shape strategy?
- Is testing integrated and scaled based on program risk?
- Is there a transition plan to deploy capabilities?
- Is there a plan to operate the capability in accordance with the DISA Service Operations Framework?
- Is there a realistic Integrated Master Schedule?
- Has the program identified and mitigated risks?

- Does the strategy satisfy the customer's requirements?
- Is the strategy designed to maximize competition?
- How will the contract type minimize risk to the government?
- Are there existing contract vehicles available for the required services? If not, should DISA develop an enterprise contract vehicle for this service?
- Does the strategy appropriately leverage contract type and objective incentives to motivate contractors to exceed minimum performance requirements?
- Have conflict-of-interest issues been addressed and eliminated or mitigation plans established?

The following information is also required for Decision Point 2 approval:

Information Required at Decision Point 2:
- Acquisition Strategy (includes Technical Analysis, Market Research, Pilot/Prototype Results, Information Support Plan, Technical Data Rights Strategy, Systems Engineering Plan, Architecture Strategy, Test and Evaluation Management Plan, and Lifecycle Sustainment Plan)
- Capability Requirements Document
- Concept of Operations
- Services Operations Annex
- Acquisition Program Baseline
- Cost Estimate
- Cost Recovery Strategy
- Acquisition Plan
- Request for Proposal and Other Contracting Docs
- Service Level Agreements (when applicable)
- Business Processes Reengineering and CRM Strategy
- Clinger-Cohen Act Compliance

The acquisition team will prepare an Acquisition Decision Memorandum (ADM) and the Decision Authority will sign it. The ADM will capture the key decisions in the meeting, any action items for the acquisition team, any guidance or deviations from policy and guidance for criteria for the next acquisition phase and deployment decision.

6.3 Configure and Adapt Phase

Activities to be performed in this phase include configuring and adapting the COTS/GOTS products for enterprise use, implementing business process reengineering activities to include CRM processes, and testing and obtaining network certification approval.

6.3.1 Analyze Gaps

While the team conducted a technical analysis in the previous phase, a gap assessment is needed once the COTS/GOTS products have been acquired. The acquisition team, in collaboration with the

86

contractor and end user, should determine if any gaps exist between the intended functionality of the COTS/GOTS capability and the program needs. If gaps are identified, the acquisition team should consider a variety of options to include alternative technical solutions, business process reengineering, and product customization. Once gaps have been identified and assessed, and solutions explored, stakeholders and decision makers can determine the way ahead based on risk, budgets, schedule, and other factors. The DISA Chief Engineers Panel (CEP) must vet the proposed technical solution prior to acquisition.

6.3.2 Configuration, Development, and Integration

Acquisitions for COTS and GOTS products will often require extensive configuration and integration with related systems, platforms, and infrastructure. The details of this should have been captured in the acquisition strategy and related program documents prior to Decision Point 2 as well as in the RFP and contract(s). DISA staff and contractors will often have shared responsibility for configuration and integration of IT capabilities for an enterprise service. DISA staff with knowledge of enterprise architectures, platforms, standards, interfaces, and mission assurance responsibilities will always be ultimately responsible. Contractors who either developed the COTS/GOTS software or provide support services will likely have the knowledge of the software details for configuration.

Roles and responsibilities must be clearly defined across all stakeholders to ensure a common understanding. The more complex or risky programs may require a more comprehensive approach to include identification and resolution of issues and consideration of likely IT environments. Teams may use collaboration software, recurring meetings, and other methods to ensure that all stakeholders are aware of the status, issues, and resolutions.

In some cases, the program/vendor team will acquire and configure the selected COTS/GOTS components and integrate them into a pilot service to demonstrate capabilities to customer representatives. These efforts are analogous to development activities and warrant close working relationships between the program office, vendor, and customer representatives to ensure that the efforts do not stray from established requirements and expectations.

Customization is distinguished from configuration and integration in that it might require modifying existing products to support DoD unique needs. Generally the DoD discourages customization of COTS products as it shifts the nature of the acquisition closer to a development effort. In the event that the enterprise service requires custom development, the acquisition team will select the appropriate development methodology (e.g., agile, incremental) most appropriate for the customization. The acquisition team should refer to Models 1 and 2 in this guide for information on agile and incremental development processes.

If the enterprise services is being acquired as a fully outsourced managed IT service, the acquisition team should follow the processes outlined in Model 8 of this guide.

Lastly, when existing services are proposed as candidates to become DoD enterprise services, the process used to adapt the capability for enterprise adoption follows a streamlined version of the enterprise services model. Streamlining may eliminate some technology assessment activities, piloting efforts, and potentially certification and accreditation.

Business Process Reengineering (BPR) is redesigning the way work is done to better support the organization's mission and reduce costs. The intent of BPR in this model is to redesign DISA business processes, to the maximum extent possible, to conform to the best practice business rules adopted by industry. In most cases, it is best to adopt the COTS/GOTS solution "out-of-the-box" rather than adapting the product to accommodate existing systems and processes.

For COTS acquisitions, additional BPR is conducted after program initiation to reengineer an organization's retained processes to match available COTS processes. New enterprise services may require reengineering of customer processes. User representative must be included in piloting and configuration activities to understand the impact on their processes. The improved service understanding will almost certainly result in new or modified service requirements. Care must be taken to prioritize these requirements according to the established governance process.

For additional information on BPR activities, reference Chapter IV, Section 5.

6.3.3 Customer Relationship Management Planning

The acquisition team should being implementing the CRM plan that was developed in the previous phase. The team should begin developing CRM processes, identifying customer engagement strategies, pricing models, SLAs, and customer service and issue resolution management processes.

For additional information on SLAs, reference Chapter IV, Section 7.

6.3.4 Conduct Testing

After completing integration and configuration activities, the government must conduct acceptance and operational testing of the service prior to a formal deployment decision. PEO test engineers, JITC testers, and operational user representatives will assess the service according to their roles and provide input to the deployment decision.

For information on how to conduct testing activities, reference Chapter IV, Section 10.

6.3.5 Conduct Pilots

The acquisition team should conduct piloting/prototyping activities as needed for risk reduction activities.

For additional information on prototypes, reference Chapter IV, Section 9.

6.3.6 Obtain Network Certification

Validation of the adapted COTS/GOTS products using an approved test plan is required to obtain network certification and add the products to the Service Catalog. A network certification is obtained through a knowledge point review and documented in a decision memorandum approved by the DA.

During configuration and integration, the service must also undergo certification and accreditation. This process may be simplified if the components of the solution are already accredited within the DoD Information Networks. Prior to piloting, the service must have at least an Interim Authority to Operate (IATO) to allow external customers to test and review the new service. Once the pilot process and testing efforts are complete, the service should obtain a full Authority to Operate (ATO) prior to deployment.

6.3.7 Certify Clinger-Cohen Act

Clinger-Cohen Act (CCA) compliance by DISA CIO is required. For additional information on CCA compliance and certification, reference Chapter IV, Section 8.

6.4 Deployment Decision(s)

Deployment Decisions(s) by the Decision Authority will review the testing and certification reports to verify that the program meets performance and functional requirements, validate that the capabilities meet the customers'/enterprises' needs, and ensure that there is a sound strategy to operate, maintain, support, and evolve the capability. A deployment decision is approved at a Deployment Readiness Review (DRR), and a DRR checklist must be completed for deployment approval.

The acquisition team should be prepared to answer the following standard questions at Deployment Decision.

Standard Questions for Deployment Decisions:
- Has sufficient testing been conducted on the program?
- Do test results show the program has been implemented based on requirements/customer needs?
- Has the program been independently validated and verified?
- Has the program completed the required elements of the deployment readiness review checklist?
- Does the program have a suitable plan to operate and sustain the capabilities with appropriate IA?
- Does the program have a suitable plan to provide patches, upgrades, and additional releases?
- Does the program have sufficient budget to meet estimated operational and sustainment costs?
- Does the organization responsible for operating the capability concur with deployment?
- Do the appropriate stakeholders agree the capability is ready to be deployed?

In addition, the following information is required for Deployment Decision approval:

Information Required at Deployment Decision(s):

- Updated Acquisition Strategy (includes Lifecycle Sustainment Plan, Information Assurance Strategy, Technical Data Rights Strategy, Information Support Plan, Item Unique Identifier Plan, Performance Management Strategy, Transition to DECC, and Support Posture)
- Operational Test and Evaluation Results (Test Report and IA Report)
- Updated Service Operations Annex
- Deployment Readiness Review Checklist
- Integrated Checklist (for network certification)
- JITC Certification
- Clinger-Cohen Act Compliance
- Acquisition Lessons Learned and Best Practices
- Authorization to Operate (ATO)
- Training and Outreach Plan
- Continuity of Operations Plan

6.4.1 Deployments

Rolling out an enterprise service to the DoD enterprise is a major undertaking that is often done via iterative deployment efforts. A comprehensive deployment plan should be developed and coordinated long before it is approved at a DRR.

Enterprise service implementations progress through three government environments. The first is a testing environment for Government Acceptance Testing, followed by a pre-production environment that supports limited end-user testing (if applicable), and last, through the production environment, which is a live environment that supports all the enterprise users. The test environment and pre-production environments are used to also identify issues and capture lessons learned. Scaling of the enterprise service is based on user demand and data center capacity. The enterprise services are installed at the DISA data centers (i.e., Enterprise Service Centers), and in some cases where users prefer a local instantiation, the service can also be deployed at the customer's local infrastructure. Initial deployments that use a diversity of enterprise and local environments offer maximum learning opportunities for issue identification and resolution.

There must be documented agreements across the program/project office, contractors/developers, IA and testing teams, and enterprise users to have clear understanding of expectations, roles and responsibilities, resources required/available, costs, schedules, and risks. The SLAs developed under the CRM strategy should identify clear expectations between the program/project office and the customer.

There must be clear accountabilities and responsibilities for coordinating the deployments, as highlighted in the DRR Checklist. Deployment activities include managing the schedules, resources, agreements, expectations, and active collaboration of stakeholders on status, issues, and resolutions.

Deployment decisions are facilitated by completing the DRR and obtaining the Chief Engineer's approval. Continual process improvement should be integrated into the deployment plan to ensure best practices and lessons learned can be applied to subsequent deployments.

6.5 Operations and Support Phase

The objectives of this phase are to operate and support the capability for the user through the end of the intended lifecycle. Additional releases and considerations for follow-on and/or subsequent technical refresh acquisitions are evaluated in this phase.

During the Operations and Support phase, the capability will be operated using the operational processes defined in the DESMF. Depending on the agreed operational concept documented as part of the Service Operations Framework, the acquisition organization may have enduring responsibilities for providing on-call technical expertise to help resolve escalated operational issues. The Services Operation Annex that was developed and updated in the previous phases provides all stakeholders with a concise reference as to how the service operates, and who is responsible for various aspects of operations. In particular, this document addresses service-specific responsibilities for executing the processes/functions of the DESMF Service Operations domain, and addresses how Command and Control (C2) of the service will be conducted.

In addition to operating the service for the user, acquisition planning for technical refresh, modernization, and/or follow-on activities begins in this phase. Analysis of subsequent requirements across the DISA portfolios should be conducted to ensure that efforts are not duplicated and the best approach is identified. If a refresh or follow-on activity is not required, the phase concludes with a decision for project disposal.

Customer feedback, performance monitoring, emerging technologies, and evolving customer requirements will drive a need for service enhancement during the operational life of the enterprise service. Regardless of the acquisition model used to initially acquire the enterprise service, these enhancements can be viewed as "mini" development activities that might include replacing existing COTS components, adding new components, reconfiguring the existing service, or if necessary modifying the existing service to meet DoD unique requirements.

Enhancement project are typically contracted for as separate contract line items or task orders to meet specific bounded requirements. Once awarded, these projects represent small instances of the same configuration and integration activities originally conducted to produce the operational system.

For more information on Operations and Support, reference Chapter IV, Section 12.

7 Continuous Capability Delivery (Model 7)

IT portfolios and programs that satisfy a long term capability requirement on a continuous basis. The requirements are focused on delivery of an ongoing capability and the overarching requirements are stable over time while derived requirements continue to evolve (Figure 12). Originally these capabilities were initially acquired via one of the other models or legacy systems. This model focuses primarily on the activities that take place after Deployment and addresses the long term nature (10 years +) of functionally related IT solutions that are in the operations and sustainment mode.

Some of the key characteristics of this acquisition model include:

- Cleary defined operational outcomes
- Regular assessment and prioritization of the operational environment and requirements
- Continuous performance monitoring and management
- Contractor is incentivized to continually deliver capabilities to optimize performance
- Development of a technical and business environment that enables smooth integration of new technologies developed internal and external to the program

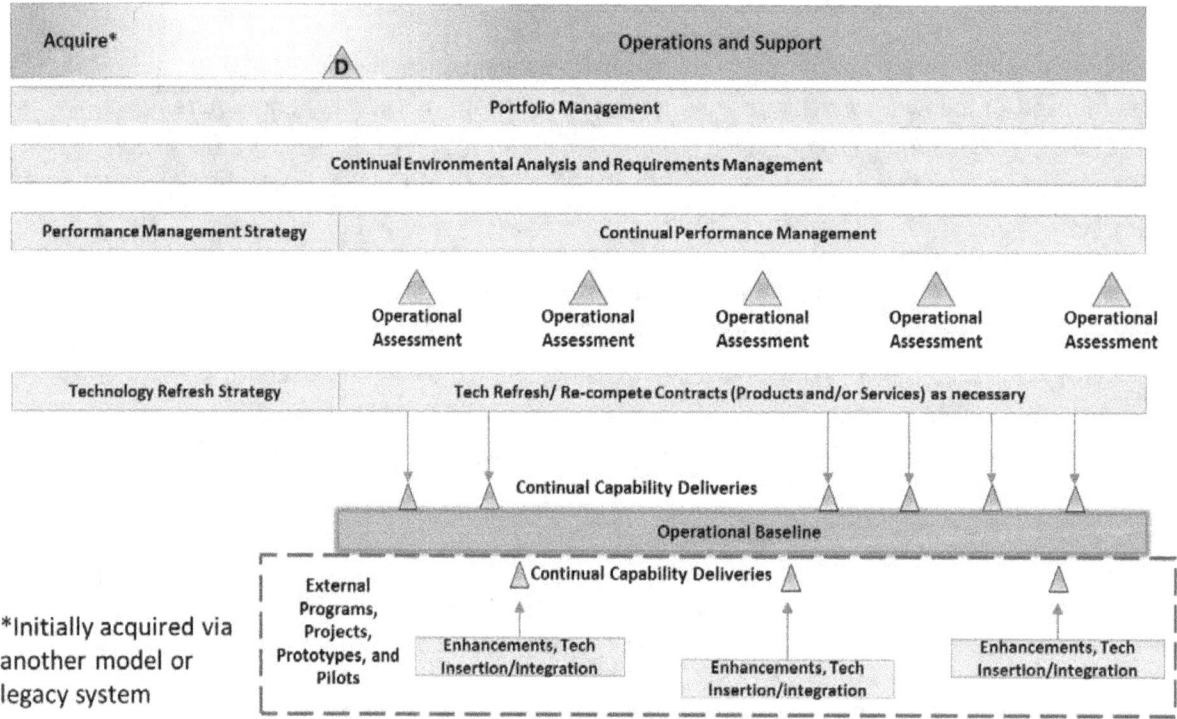

Figure 12 Continuous Capability Delivery Model Process View

7.1 Portfolio Management

Key decision points for this type of IT acquisition are not traditional milestone/phase decisions but are focused on long term requirements management, tracking/assessing performance, adjusting plans based on dynamic priorities, and continuing to ensure delivery of current and cost efficient services/products. This type of acquisition could be a single product or service (HBSS), but more often is a set of solutions that together address the scope of the requirement (i.e. spectrum management, cyber analytics, etc.). This model provides a cohesive means to manage a collection of IT products and services that together meet the requirements for a long term functional capability. Standard portfolio management practices should apply. These include allocating requirements to programs/projects, periodic portfolio assessments, monitoring operational outcomes against portfolio objectives, and dynamic replanning to optimize portfolio outcomes.

7.1.1 Requirements Management

Typically requirements for this type of acquisition are stable, documented, long term, high level requirements with dynamic requirements impacting the solution below the capability level. For example, HBSS provides an ongoing security solution and the requirement for a secure environment is fairly stable. However, on a regular basis the dynamic nature of the threat necessitates that the product continue to evolve to maintain the required levels of security. The premise for this model is that 85-100% of the capability has been delivered and the enhancements required to keep pace with the threat or need can be addressed within the established program/portfolio baseline. Requirements are allocated to programs/projects within the portfolio and the ability to continue to meet those requirements is periodically assessed. New or modified requirements are vetted, prioritized, and validated with stakeholders, to include cost/benefit trade-offs.

7.1.2 Performance Management

As an acquisition in operations and sustainment, continual performance monitoring is expected. The program or portfolio should have a documented set of performance requirements from multiple perspectives to include operational support for the user, network operations, security, system, service levels, etc. These require a structured annual assessment, which may be a consolidation of multiple assessments, to ensure that the performance continues to meet expectations over time. For major Acquisition of Service, an annual operational assessment is required (circular A-11, DISA AOS guidance). From a DISA perspective, products and services need to meet performance targets and expectations through proactive monitoring, in addition to feedback from users. The intent is to identify potential performance issues and have the opportunity to resolve them before they result in significant impact to customers. Ideally performance is monitored through use of tools that provide summary metrics, alerts and dashboards for rapid identification of potential performance issues. A structured assessment takes all sources of information into account to provide a holistic perspective.

In addition to operational and outcome performance monitoring, it is important to monitor the program/project execution for efficiency and sustainability. Every program and project within the

portfolio, needs to have allocated cost, schedule and performance parameters. There should be a structured process for execution review to ensure continued ability to meet requirements with existing resources.

7.2   Technology Refresh/Recompete

Technology refresh is required not only to maintain capability, but more importantly to constrain costs. As technology used in solutions and services gets further from the commercial offering, the costs for sustainment continue to increase. The activities and costs for technology refresh need to be built into the program baseline at a level that meets industry standards. Often technology refresh is not sufficiently resourced in order to allocate more funding in the portfolio to capability enhancements. This adds risk, cost, and impacts performance, but because it is difficult to quantify, it is often a target of cuts. Each program/portfolio should have a technology refresh plan that addresses all components, software, hardware, integration, etc. At the portfolio and program level, analysis should be ongoing to monitor technology trends and standard technology refresh cycles. The technology refresh plan should reference that analysis and should demonstrate how the technology refresh meets performance requirements.

Recompeting the product or service as contract periods of performance end is another form of technology refresh. As the commercial offerings evolve, there are more opportunities to reduce costs through buying services. Over time the commercial service offerings change, the scope of capability increases, and costs decrease. While recompeting enterprise level services has a potential significant user impact, it also has potential for significant benefit. These opportunities need to be built into the program baseline with all the appropriate decision points. Typically a recompete is initiated with a review and validation of requirements and an acquisition strategy kickoff. The acquisition strategy for a recompete should include reconsidering the roles and responsibilities of the government and contractor based on updated market research. This includes the range of potential alternatives from government owned and operated, to contractor owned and operated. In addition, it should include reassessing the scope of work, whether to expand the scope of the contract vehicles beyond the portfolio, opportunities to lower costs, and alternatives for partitioning the work to improve competition. Since the procurement cycle can take up to two years for a major contract award, the required activities need to be built into the schedule in order to minimize impact to users and maximize continuity.

7.3   Enhancements and Technology Insertion

Since requirements are not static for any IT acquisition, even programs in sustainment will continue to need to deliver capability improvements and to address a changing threat environment. For portfolios or programs of this type, the majority of capability has been delivered and enhancements are typically within the scope of existing program/portfolio requirements. The baseline needs to include resource scope and schedule activities planned in to accommodate enhancements and technology insertion opportunities. Even if there is no expected change in requirements, as technology evolves over a long

term program life cycle, investments are required for insertion of new technology that may not only provide significant performance improvements but also significant cost savings. The scale of enhancements and technology insertion should not exceed the scope of about 10% of the total program capability scope. Because of the small scale of enhancements, the program/portfolio continues to remain in the phase of operations and sustainment. Unless planned for sunset, all major IT programs in sustainment are expected to continue to maintain pace with technology, evolve the solution to continue to meet requirements, and incorporate advancements that are needed to optimize efficiency and reduce costs.

While it is often not clear in advance what the future enhancements will be needed or what new technology opportunities will evolve, it has been proven through execution of many IT programs that assuming no enhancements is not realistic. In addition, the work and cost of setting up a new follow-on program has limited benefit if existing sustainment programs can stay current with technology and continue to meet requirements. The budget and procurement cycles are not dynamic enough to respond to changing IT environment, so flexibility needs to be built in at the program or portfolio level. In many cases, the research and development required to leverage new technology or meet an evolving requirement may be done outside the scope of a program or portfolio (JCTD, pilot, project, etc.). Therefore, planning flexibility in the sustainment phase should include both small capability enhancements and transition of capabilities or technology into the existing sustainment portfolio. This would typically require planned cycles for future integration and testing.

DISA IT Acquisition Guidebook

8   Managed IT Services (Model 8)

The managed IT services model (see Figure 13) is used to capitalize on the benefits of managed services provided by an outside service or existing operational service provider. The contractor or service provider is the systems integrator, owns hardware/software, and manages configuration, otherwise known as contractor-owned and -operated services. All service acquisitions are subject to DoD 5000.02, Enclosure 9, Acquisition of Services policies and instructions, as well as CAE Guideline 001 on Acquisition of Services.

Some of the key characteristics of this acquisition model include:

- Defining the service that is being acquired.
- Analyzing minimum government data rights requirements.
- Clearly identifying transition support requirements.
- Developing a strategy for capacity/scalability management.
- Identifying the impact on vendor pricing when capacity needs to be scaled up and down.

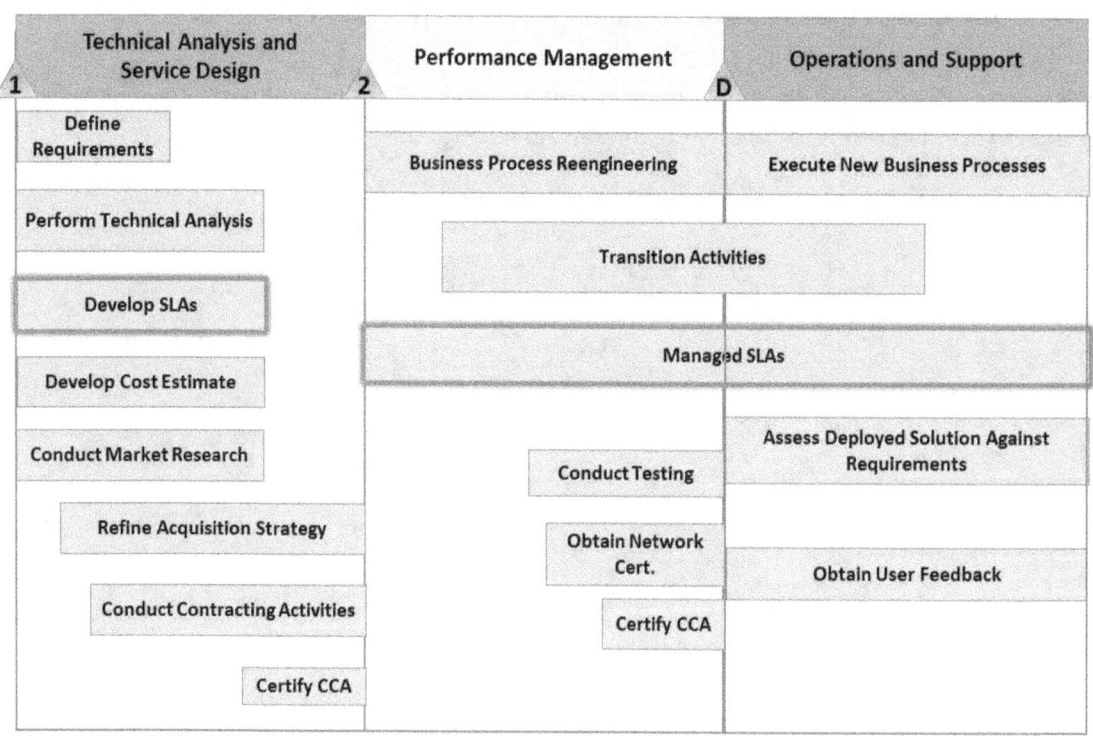

Figure 13 Managed IT Services Model Process View

Managed Service Case Study: Defense Connect Online (DCO)

DCO was acquired as the second offering of a collaboration service under the Net Centric Enterprise Services (NCES) program. Tailoring the managed IT service model somewhat, DISA acquired two competing collaboration capabilities. This strategy was intended to reward service vendors based on usage and thus incentivize frequent service enhancements. Users would, in theory, shift between the tools as improvements were made, eliminating the need for a formal continuity of operations (COOP) plan for either service. Staggering the managed service contract awards would ensure a capability was always available.

Though both services performed well, users clearly preferred DCO and feedback indicated that users would prefer a single capability with built-in continuity versus training and operating on two different enterprise collaboration tools. The first service was discontinued, and a DCO continuity of operations enhancement project was undertaken to meet established JROC-approved user requirements. For this project, the vendor delivered a DoD unique synchronization and failover solution based on similar capabilities from their commercial cloud offering. The acquisition model for this continuity project could best be described as an integration of COTS/GOTS into the existing service (Model 5), but also with some custom scripting development to support DoD unique requirements (Model 1). During sustainment, the integration responsibility, ownership, and operations functions remained with the vendor.

Additional service enhancements related to PKI credentials and traffic balancing between sites followed similar models, and the vender was also responsible for incorporating new commercial versions as they become available.

8.1 Technical Analysis and Service Design Phase

The objectives of the technical analysis and service design phase are to engage with industry, identify services available, design requirements based on industry capabilities, and develop strategies to maximize competition. The activities in this phase—shaping requirements, defining the technical baseline, and conducting technical analysis of services available, cost estimates, market research, contracting, etc.—are performed in parallel and tightly aligned. All of the processes influence each other and will help the acquisition team develop the optimal strategy for the acquisition.

Under a managed IT service, the focus shifts from buying, implementing, and managing the software application to establishing and managing the government and vendor relationship. Activities to be performed in this phase continue building on the documents and decisions from the initiation phase. The requirements are refined and finalized in this phase using the analyses of alternatives from the initiation phase. The following activities, documents, and plans must be executed, developed, and completed/approved.

8.1.1 Define Requirements

The team will use the high-level requirements identified in the initiation phase to finalize the requirements for the RFP. Under a managed IT service contract, the government should describe

requirements as performance objectives and/or outcomes. A Statement of Objectives (SOO) is the recommended strategy for documenting a managed IT service requirement. Because the government is acquiring the full end-to-end capability as a fully outsourced capability, the acquisition team should develop SLAs in parallel to the requirements development process.

All members of the acquisition team should be strongly engaged in the requirements definition process, especially the requirements (user) community. Defining requirements begins with the drafting of a statement of the user's need, including the level of performance and availability the end-user would like to have. This statement should define the operational need for the item, including the intended application, and should also define the desired support services, such as training, testing, maintenance, and repair services. Stating requirements in terms of objectives, rather than specifying exactly how the item should be manufactured or the service performed, allows for a greater flexibility in determining the appropriate solution. Stating the requirements in terms of objectives will also facilitate the development of the Statement of Objectives/Performance Work Statement in the contracting phase.

The acquisition team should also take into consideration how DISA will use the managed IT service. An additional consideration is deciding if the managed IT services will also be a service available to the enterprise (e.g., acquired by DISA for DISA-specific use but can also be made available to DoD partners) or an enterprise service (e.g., acquired by DISA but intended for DoD-wide use). It is important to make these considerations early in the acquisition process to ensure that the requirements document accurately reflects the intended scope of the effort, with the flexibility to expand the contract scope if needed.

The requirements should identify the full life-cycle needs of the program, from implementation, to maintenance, to disposal. The clear definition of hardware and software interfaces is another factor to consider in developing requirements and acquisition strategies when several subsystems will be linked within a single system. Periodically, software interfaces may need to be redesigned to keep up with evolving commercial technology and improve total system performance. For managed IT services, the government should develop acquisition strategies that make contractors responsible for managing software interfaces and that encourage the seamless integration of technology upgrades into existing systems.

For additional information on Requirements, reference Chapter IV, Section 1.

> **Key Questions:**
> - Does the PWS/SOO identify measureable performance objectives and outcomes?
> - Is the PWS/SOO constructed to allow the contractor(s) to deliver the service by following its own best practices?
> - Is there a definition of the service that is being acquired (specs, SLAs)?
> - Will this managed IT service be offered as a service available to the enterprise?
> - Will this managed IT service be offered as an enterprise service? (if so, enterprise service questions from Model 3 may also be applicable)

> • Is the requirement defined in terms of end-user experience?

8.1.2 Develop SLAs

SLAs are especially important under a managed IT service acquisition because the acquisition is not focused on the delivery of a product but on establishing and managing the government and vendor relationship. SLAs are used to document and enforce contract terms and control the quality of performance.

Under a managed IT service acquisition, it is recommended that SLAs be used to cover, at a minimum, the following areas:

- Key contact information
- Hours of operation and location of services
- Escalation process
- Issue response and resolution times
- Uptime and performance guarantees
- Standard maintenance windows
- Service credits
- Disaster recovery and business continuity
- Termination
- Maintenance and custom support
- Data protection
- Cost

For more information on recommended SLAs, refer to the DoD Enterprise Software Initiative whitepaper on Best Practices for Negotiating a Cloud-Based Software Contract or Cloud SLA Considerations for the Government Consumer from the MITRE Systems Engineering Institute (SLA recommendations in this paper are not exclusively limited to cloud-based acquisitions).

For additional information on SLAs, reference Chapter IV, Section 7.

Key Questions:
- Are sufficient rates available for operational data to validate SLAs?
- Do the performance objectives align with industry best practices and standards?

8.1.3 Develop a Technical Baseline

The core of a technical baseline is primarily the description, design, and decomposition of the system's hardware, software, and integration. For a managed IT service, because the government does not own any hardware and software, the technical baseline should list capabilities, functional requirements, security requirements, and technical requirements.

For additional information on technical baselines, reference Chapter IV, Section 2.1.

> **Key Question:**
> - Is there a comprehensive, complete, current, and independently verified technical baseline aligned to the cost baseline, requirements, budgets, schedules, and enterprise architectures?
> - Has a sufficient technical/cost tradeoff analysis been conducted?

8.1.4 Develop Cost Estimate

The acquisition team should use the technical baseline to develop a cost estimate for the program. The cost estimate for a managed IT service acquisition can become complicated due to the differences in vendor pricing structures and service levels. Working with the CFE office or obtaining cost support to develop a cost estimate is recommended.

From a managed IT services standpoint, the acquisition team should use market research to identify different commercial pricing structures for the required service. In some cases, the pricing can be based on a per-seat basis or a monthly subscription fees. Additionally, the program should factor into the estimate what happens to the cost when capacity needs to be scaled up and down (e.g., discount pricing available at higher thresholds).

A detailed cost estimate containing a breakdown by cost element anticipated in the performance of the contract is required for services. For pricing purposes, this cost estimate should include additional services provided by DISA. Reference Appendix 6 of the DAG and the DISA Cost Manual for additional information regarding cost estimates for service acquisitions.

For additional information on cost estimates, reference Chapter IV, Section 4.

> **Key Questions:**
> - How does the cost estimate account for the adjustment of capacity when it needs to be scaled up and down?
> - Is the pricing metric for the service determined by the number of users? Is the metric per unique/seat users, concurrent, or only active users?
> - Does the provider also charge for technical support users who are not using the software application but need ad hoc access to it?

8.1.5 Conduct Market Research

The acquisition team should continue with the market research that was conducted in the initiation phase.

Through market research and industry engagement, the acquisition team should have a list of potential managed IT solutions. This candidate list will often offer a wide variety of features, capabilities, risks, and opportunities. The evaluation of candidate products will help shape the final requirements and scope of the program and releases. As the acquisition team performs the technical analysis, they should actively engage industry to identify and understand features, ratings, costs, risks, and more. Collaborating with independent experts who review these services is another valuable source of information. Industry engagement must be done in accordance with contracting officer guidance.

The market research for managed IT services should analyze both the different technical solutions available as well as the variety of vendors that can deliver the required service. The acquisition team is encouraged to use a Request for Information (RFI) or use an industry day to understand the breadth and depth of capabilities available in the marketplace to fulfill the government needs. If the managed IT service required is for a service that is widely offered in the commercial marketplace (e.g., cloud services), the RFI should request standard pricing information and current SLAs as part of communication with vendors. The acquisition team is encouraged to communicate with vendors as part of the market research process with support and guidance from the contracting office.

For additional information on market research, see Chapter IV, Section 6.2.

Key Questions:
- Has market research been conducted to identify different technical solutions available to meet requirements?
- Has market research been conducted to identify multiple vendors that can deliver this service?
- Has the acquisition team obtained current pricing structures and SLAs as part of the market research activity?

8.1.6 Refine Acquisition Strategy

The team will continue to build on the high-level acquisition strategy developed in the initiation phase. The acquisition strategy should define the contracting strategy, describe the overall strategy to define and manage SLAs, manage performance-based contracts, develop and maintain cost estimates, plan and execute transition activities, conduct testing, obtain network certification, and perform operations and support activities. For a managed IT service, the acquisition strategy should also address how the program plans to absorb frequent capability updates from a provider that uses a continuous delivery model. DISA should address under what conditions the provider's updates and upgrades require testing and certification, and how the program plans to absorb frequent capability updates and upgrades to the software that are controlled by the provider. For a managed IT service, the strategy to test the service prior to Go-Live, conduct transition, and manage SLAs is of particular importance.

For additional information on acquisition strategies, reference Chapter IV, Section 3.

Key Questions:
- Does the contract have the proper transition support requirements?
- How will testing be conducted for the managed IT service?
- What level of government involvement is required for testing?

8.1.7 Conduct Contracting Activities

Managed IT service acquisitions should be acquired via a performance-based service contract. If using a SOO, the RFP should request the offerors to develop a PWS and propose a QASP with proposed SLAs. A well-defined PWS and QASP will guide the business strategy in determining the appropriate contract type, incentive arrangements, and type of acquisition supported by analysis of market research (e.g.,

existing DISA contract vehicle, other agency's contract vehicle, small business set-aside, Federal Supply Schedule, commercial contracting). The Acquisition Plan is usually required for a new contract effort and must address the technical, business, management and other significant considerations to implement the approved Acquisition Strategy and must follow the format prescribed by FAR Part 7.105. In many cases, a combined Acquisition Strategy/Acquisition Plan can be used for a service acquisition in lieu of separate documents. When using an existing contract vehicle, the acquisition team should check with the contracting office if an Acquisition Plan is required.

The source selection strategy should be based on best value and the evaluation of the offerors' SLAs should be an important evaluation criterion. For managed IT services that are widely offered in the commercial marketplace, it is recommended that offerors be given the opportunity to propose their standard pricing model (versus a government structured pricing model) that will form Section B (Pricing Schedule) of the contract. The acquisition team should work with the CFE office or obtain outside cost estimating support to help evaluate the offeror's price proposals.

When negotiating a managed IT services contract, the payment terms need to be carefully analyzed. Sometimes the hosting, software licensing/use rights and maintenance fees are bundled together into one monthly or annual fee. As a result, the government is required to start paying for the service at contract start, even if it may not be used in production yet. For instance, the program may need time to setup data integration, but the provider may still charge full usage price. Therefore, it is recommended that the acquisition team only commit to the number of users that are needed upfront and ramp up usage thereafter as demand warrants. The acquisition team should also check if the managed IT service provider has a sandbox or proof-of-concept environment where the government can become familiar with the software, product, or services at little to no charge before signing a contract for a specific term and number of users.

Contract Recommendations (all recommendations may not be applicable in all managed IT service acquisitions but represent a good list of considerations that should be made in the contract negotiation process)
- Clearly identify all of the functionality that the government is paying for from the provider to ensure they do not degrade functionality over time. One good way to memorialize this in the contract is to attach a functionality matrix as an appendix to the contract.
- List all additional and optional fees in the contract, such as additional storage fees and custom reports.
- The contract should clearly identify who owns any customizations or enhancements, especially if the government pays for them as a "work product" developed solely for government-use.
- Include language that states who owns data during all of its lifecycle, including when data is transferred or exchanged (data in transit) and during storage (data at rest).
- Include language regarding who bears the risk for loss of data in transit.
- Define and confirm a process regarding regular backup of data on government premises.

- Define what the contractor's responsibilities are in the event of 1) a security breach (e.g. ensure they provide an immediate notice if data may be compromised); 2) an outage; and 3) termination (e.g., ensure that the provider will cooperate with the return of government data in a format and manner previously agreed, and with no additional fees for the return of data). Operational stakeholders should be consulted to ensure that contractor operational actions are integrated with the DISA Service Operations Framework, and that service operational status is appropriately up-channeled to DISA.

- Confidentiality language relative to the DoD and the Federal Information Security Management Act (FISMA).

- Obtain detailed information about the service provider's security processes and procedures, including data flow diagrams.

- Ensure that the DoD is involved in reviewing and determining what data the provider will store and what layers of security need to be in place. This includes making sure all applicable Information Assurance (IA) Policy and regulatory documentation is made part of the agreement reference list.

- Confirm how data access will be limited, including review of the different user permission roles offered, the various accessibility parameters for each role, and the administrator's access rights (e.g., ensure that all users' actions can be tracked).

- Ensure the government has the right to audit the provider's facilities and documentation to verify that minimum security levels are in place and being enforced, including confirmation that Government data is located where it should be and not being sent to a third party or being intermingled with other clients' data.

- Ask for third-party reports regarding penetration and vulnerability results for provider's hosting environment.

- Include language confirming the provider's data storage period and data destruction policy.

- Include language confirming the provider's business continuity plan, specifying redundancy requirements to include, at a minimum, data backup and recovery methods/infrastructure/ processes. Also, have the provider certify that they will participate with the government in disaster recovery testing at specific time intervals (e.g., once every two years) without charge.

- Even though providers may lock the government in for a specific contract term and minimum number of users, ensure the ability to terminate for cause, including a continued lack of uptime— specific criteria should be identified in the SLA.

- Ensure payment terms are clear and confirm that the provider cannot immediately shut off services for late or disputed invoices.

- Include a transition CLIN for both transition-in as well as transition-out at the end of the contract period.

- Include a liquidated damages clause to allow the government to collect dollars per calendar day for delay when the contractor fails to deliver services on time.

- Include the option to extend services clause to allow the contract to be extended for up to 6 months in case there are issues with contract recompete and/or contract transition.

- Include the continuity of services clause to ensure that the contractor agrees to furnish phase-in training and exercise its best efforts and cooperation to effect an orderly and efficient transition to a successor.

For additional information on contracting, reference Chapter IV, Section 6.

Key Questions:
- What is the impact on vendor pricing when capacity needs to be scaled up and down?
- How frequently does the vendor plan to conduct performance or system upgrades?
- What is the process to determine if the upgrade will require action from DISA?
- Has contract language been written into the contract to allow for the retrieval of government data (if necessary) in a common data format?
- Does the contract include performance incentives and disincentives?
- Does the government retain ownership of government data?
- Can the government retrieve the data at the end of contract life?

8.1.8 Certify Clinger-Cohen Act

Clinger-Cohen Act (CCA) compliance by DISA CIO is required. For additional information on CCA compliance and certification, reference Chapter IV, Section 8.

8.1.9 Peer Review

All service contracts with an estimated value of $1 billion or more, including options (and any program designated special interest by AT&L), are required to complete a Defense Procurement and Acquisition Policy (DPAP) Peer Review. Additionally, for services that are below the $1 billion threshold, similar reviews should be conducted within DISA to ensure best practices in the acquisition of services. To align with DoD's Better Buying Power Initiative, strategic sourcing goals and metrics (such as utilization rates) should be included in the Peer Review Process to allow visibility at the department level.

Competitive procurements have three pre-award phases:
1. Prior to issuance of the solicitation
2. Prior to request for final proposal revisions
3. Prior to contract award

For non-competitive procurements, pre-award peer reviews shall be conducted at the pre- and post-business clearance phases.

Pre-award peer reviews assess the following elements:
1. The process was well understood by both government and industry.
2. Source selection was carried out in accordance with the Source Selection Plan and RFP.
3. The Source Selection Evaluation Board evaluation was clearly documented.
4. The Source Selection Advisory Council advisory panel recommendation was clearly documented.

5. The Source Selection Authority decision was clearly derived from the conduct of the source selection process.
6. All source selection documentation is consistent with the Section M evaluation criteria.
7. The business arrangement.

Post-award peer reviews shall assess the following elements:
1. Contract performance in terms of cost, schedule, and requirements.
2. Use of contracting mechanisms, including the use of competition, the contract structure and type, the definition of contract requirements, cost or pricing methods, the award and negotiation of task orders, and management and oversight mechanism.
3. The contractor's use, management, and oversight of subcontractors/
4. The staffing of contract management and oversight function.
5. The extent of any pass-through charges and excessive pass-through charges by the contractor (as defined in DFARS 252.215-7004).

For contracts under which one contractor provides oversight for services performed by other contractors:
1. Extent of the DoD component's reliance on the contractor to perform acquisition functions closely associated with inherently governmental functions as defined in 10 U.S.C. 2383(b)(3).
2. The financial interest of any prime contractor performing acquisition functions described in paragraph 1 in any contract or subcontract with regard to which the contractor provided advice or recommendations to the agency.

For more information, visit the DPAP website for processes for completing the Peer Review process.

8.2 Decision Point 2

At Decision Point 2, the Decision Authority reviews analyses and strategies to acquire the capabilities and verifies program affordability to meet validated requirements within the available budget. The Decision Authority approves the release of the RFP or contract award at Decision Point 2.

In addition to the key questions identified above, the acquisition team should be prepared to answer the following standard questions at Decision Point 2:

Standard Questions for Decision Point 2:
• Are the program requirements validated and prioritized?
• Have rigorous cost estimates been conducted?
• Is the program affordable within the available budget?
• Does the contract strategy address risk, incentives, data rights, and competition across the lifecycle?
• Does the team actively engage industry to shape strategy?
• Is test integrated and scaled based on program risk?
• Is there a transition plan to deploy capabilities?

- Is there a plan to operate the capability in accordance with the DISA Service Operations Framework?
- Is there a realistic Integrated Master Schedule?
- Has the program identified and mitigated risks?
- Is the strategy designed to maximize competition?
- How will the contract type minimize risk to the government?
- Are there existing contract vehicles available for the required services? If not, should DISA develop an enterprise contract vehicle for this service?
- Does the strategy appropriately leverage contract type and objective incentives to motivate contractors to exceed minimum performance requirements?
- Have conflict-of-interest issues been addressed and eliminated or mitigation plans established?

The following information is also required for Decision Point 2 approval:

Information Required at Decision Point 2:
- Acquisition Strategy (includes Technical Analysis, Market Research, Information Support Plan, Technical Data Rights Strategy, Architecture Strategy , and Lifecycle Sustainment Plan)
- Capability Requirements Document
- Concept of Operations
- Services Operations Annex
- Acquisition Program Baseline
- Cost Estimate
- Acquisition Plan
- Request for Proposal and Other Contracting Docs
- Service Level Agreements (when applicable)
- Business Processes Reengineering (when applicable)
- Clinger-Cohen Act Compliance

The acquisition team will prepare an Acquisition Decision Memorandum (ADM) and the Decision Authority will sign it. . The ADM will capture the key decisions in the meeting, any action items for the acquisition team, and any guidance or deviations from policy and guidance for criteria for the next acquisition phase and deployment decision.

8.3 Configure and Demonstrate Phase

The objectives of this phase are to complete the acquisition of the managed IT service, complete integration/configuration, and adapt the service to operate within the DISA enterprise.

Activities to be performed in this phase include performing the configuration of the managed IT service, testing and obtaining the necessary certifications and documents to add to the DISA enterprise, and offering the adapted product to customers.

8.3.1 Business Process Reengineering

Business Process Reengineering (BPR) is redesigning the way work is done to better support the organization's mission and reduce costs. The intent of BPR in this model is to redesign DISA business processes, to the maximum extent possible, to conform to the best practice business rules adopted by industry. The acquisition team, to the maximum extent practicable, should adapt to the managed IT providers commercial processes.

For additional information on BPR, reference Chapter IV, Section 5.

8.3.2 Plan Transition Activities

A major challenge associated with the vendor managed IT service model is a transition to a replacement service. Because the vendor owns the service, DISA cannot simply recompete the support contracts and continue the service. Instead, a replacement capability must be fully competed with an ownership model that allows the government to minimize user impact of service transitions. In breaking from the historical government system ownership and integration role, managed services can challenge program offices to create thoughtful transition plans.

To ensure success of the service, the transition of the program from acquisition to operation is critical. Sufficient resources from the acquisition team should be allocated to contract management to ensure effective and efficient performance throughout the life of the contract.

The program office should host a formal kick-off meeting or post-award conference with the contractor to establish a foundation for a solid relationship and good communication and to achieve mutual understanding of contract requirements.

As part of the preparation for a new acquisition, it recommended that the acquisition team implement a Transition Planning Team that is responsible for monitoring the Contractor's Transition-In Plan. This transition team will participate in scheduled meetings with the contractor team to discuss transition topics to include facilities, GFE, contract deliverables, and contactor personnel. The team will review the contractor awardee's submitted plan versus the government provided items for completeness. Upon award start date, the contractor will work with the assigned government POC (Program Manager, Contracting Officer's Technical Representative, or designee) to ensure that actions are executed in accordance with the contractor's plan.

8.3.3 Manage SLAs

SLAs must be applied consistently, maintained, and updated throughout the contract period of performance to ensure that performance objectives are achieved effectively. All SLAs supporting a particular effort should be managed collectively, and interdependencies should be identified and managed. To form a "meeting of the minds" between parties who may have competing agendas, SLAs should not be applied exclusively as a transactional and computer-generated communication of performance. SLAs should be applied as a mechanism for managing how the provider and government

are expected to communicate and coordinate with one another. Measuring SLA conformance and reporting results are important aspects of the SLA process that help to ensure long-term consistency and results. In general, any major component of an SLA should be measurable, and a measurement methodology should be put in place prior to SLA implementation.

Because SLA administration and management can be resource-intensive, government organizations should review SLAs periodically to ensure that the stated performance requirements are still essential to achievement of overarching outcomes.

8.3.4 Conduct Testing

The government must conduct acceptance and operational testing of the service prior to a formal deployment decision. PEO test engineers, JITC testers, and operational user representatives will assess the service according to their roles and provide input to the deployment decision.

For additional information on testing, reference Chapter IV, Section 10.

8.3.5 Obtain Network Certification

Validation of the managed IT service using an approved test plan is required to obtain network certification. A network certification is obtained through a knowledge point review and documented in a decision memorandum approved by the DA.

During configuration and integration, the service must also undergo certification and accreditation. This process may be simplified if the components of the solution are already accredited within the DoD Information Networks. Prior to piloting, the service must have at least an Interim Authority to Operate (IATO) to allow external customers to test and review the new service. Once the pilot process and testing efforts are complete, the service should obtain a full Authority to Operate (ATO) prior to deployment.

8.3.6 Certify Clinger-Cohen Act

Clinger-Cohen Act (CCA) compliance by DISA CIO is required. For additional information on CCA compliance and certification, reference Chapter IV, Section 8.

8.4 Deployment Decision(s)

Deployment Decisions(s) by the Decision Authority will review the testing and certification reports to verify that the program meets performance requirements, validate that the capabilities meet the operational sponsor / enterprise's needs, and ensure that there is a sound strategy to operate, maintain, support, and evolve the capability.

The acquisition team should be prepared to answer the following standard questions at Deployment Decision:

Standard Questions for Deployment Decisions:

108

- Has sufficient testing been conducted on the program?
- Do test results show the program has been implemented based on requirements/customer needs?
- Has the program been independently validated and verified?
- Has the program completed the required elements of the integrated checklist?
- Does the program have a suitable plan to operate and sustain the capabilities with appropriate IA?
- Does the program have a suitable plan to provide patches, upgrades, and additional releases?
- Does the program have sufficient budget to meet estimated operational and sustainment costs?
- Do the appropriate stakeholders agree the capability is ready to be deployed?

Additionally, the following information is required for Deployment Decision approval:

Information Required at Deployment Decision(s):
- Updated Acquisition Strategy (includes Lifecycle Sustainment Plan, Information Assurance Strategy, Technical Data Rights Strategy, Information Support Plan, Item Unique Identifier Plan, Performance Management Strategy, Transition to DECC, and Support Posture)
- Integrated Checklist
- Updated Services Operations Annex
- JITC Certification
- Clinger-Cohen Act Compliance
- Acquisition Lessons Learned and Best Practices
- Authorization to Operate (ATO)

8.5 Operations and Support Phase

The objectives of this phase are to operate and support the capability through the end of the intended lifecycle.

During the Operations and Support phase, the capability will be operated using the operational processes defined in the Defense Enterprise Service Management Framework. Depending on the agreed operational concept documented as part of the Service Operations Framework, the acquisition organization may have enduring responsibilities for providing on-call technical expertise to help resolve escalated operational issues.

In addition to operating the service, acquisition planning for technical refresh, modernization and/or follow-on activities begins in this phase. Analysis of subsequent requirements across the DISA portfolios should be conducted to ensure that efforts are not duplicated and the best approach is identified. If a refresh or follow-on activity is not required, the phase concludes with a decision for project disposal.

For more information on Operations and Support, reference Chapter IV, Section 12.

9   IT Support Services (Model 9)

The IT support services model (see Figure 14) is used for IT support services solutions that provide DISA operational capability such as help desk, network management, program support services, transport services, and operating equipment and facilities. All service acquisitions are subject to DoDI 5000.02, Enclosure 9, Acquisition of Services policies and instructions as well as to CAE Guideline 001 on Acquisition of Services.

*Note: In anticipation of USD(AT&L) health assessments of department-wide service acquisitions, measureable tripwire metrics should be established to effectively assess the service acquisition process within DISA. Metrics to consider are number of days Federal Procurement Database System – Next Generation (FPDS-NG) data was recorded past deadlines or the number of contract modifications within 30 days of award. Additionally, metrics may be established to evaluate the degree of effective competition within service acquisitions to baseline appropriate competition goals for future acquisitions.

Key characteristics of this acquisition model include:
- Describing service requirements as end outcomes to make them measurable.
- Defining the performance objectives, standards, and incentives.
- Developing a strategy to maximize competition.
- Using performance-based practices.
- Identifying discriminating evaluation factors and subfactors to enable the selection of contractor(s) capable of providing the required outcomes.

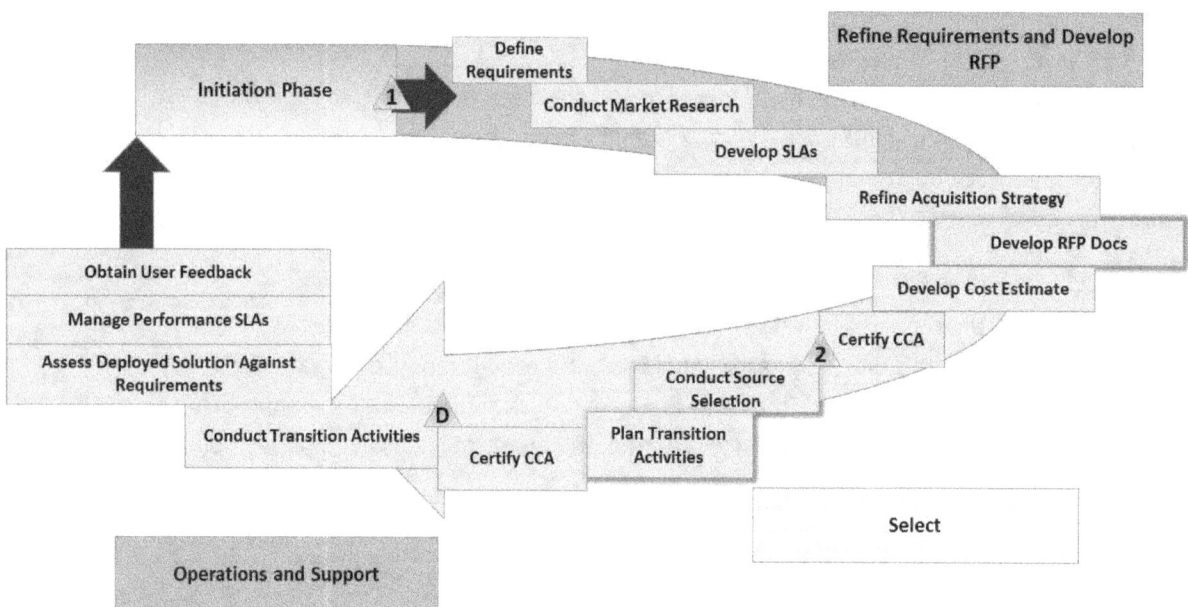

Figure 14 . IT Support Services Model Process View

9.1 Refine Requirements & Develop RFP Phase

The objectives of this phase are to evaluate the feasibility of the selected service, conduct additional market research and continue shaping the acquisition strategy to acquire the service, and prepare the request for proposal package.

Activities to be performed in this phase continue building on the documents and decisions from the initiation phase. The acquisition team should engage the DISA Procurement and Logistics Directorate (PLD) as early as possible to collaboratively develop the acquisition strategy and RFP documents. As soon as possible after identifying a need to acquire services, hold an acquisition strategy meeting, also called an Integrated Product Team (IPT). The attendees should include the person responsible for managing the program or project, contracting representative, legal advisor, potential evaluation team members, and necessary subject matter experts and others as needed.

Key Questions:
- Are the requirements validated and clearly defined?
- Are all the appropriate stakeholders engaged?

9.1.1 Market Research Report

This activity should build on the market research that was completed in the initiation phase. Good market research builds a solid foundation for the acquisition strategy and will help shape the development of the requirements. The acquisition team should consider posting a Source Sought Notice or Request for Information to gain additional insight into the commercial marketplace and commercial contractor capabilities. Before any documents such as the performance work statement are developed, market research should be conducted to obtain information about alternative solutions that may be available from the marketplace today. Once the requirement has been thoroughly analyzed, market research is also useful in developing, validating, and refining the Performance Requirements Summary for the performance work statement. Market research also allows the Government to assess if there is adequate competition in the marketplace to move forward with a competitive acquisition strategy.

For additional information on market research, reference Chapter IV, Section 6.2.

Key Question:
- Did the team actively engage industry to shape strategy?
- Does the market research support the need for competition?

9.1.2 Define Requirements

The team will use the high-level requirements identified in the initiation phase to finalize the requirements for the RFP. It is DoD policy that in order to maximize performance, innovation, and competition, often at a savings, performance-based strategies for the acquisition of services should be

used wherever possible. To be considered performance-based, an acquisition should contain, at a minimum, the following elements:

1. **Performance work statement**—Describes the requirement in terms of measurable outcomes rather than by means of prescriptive methods.
2. **Measurable performance standards**— Defines what is considered acceptable performance to determine whether performance outcomes have been met.
3. **Remedies**—Describes procedures that address how to manage performance that does not meet performance standards. While not mandatory, incentives should be used, where appropriate, to encourage performance that will exceed performance standards. Remedies and incentives complement each other.
4. **Performance Assessment Plan**—Describes how contractor performance will be measured and assessed against performance standards. (Quality Assurance Plan or Quality Assurance Surveillance Plan described below).

Teams capturing requirements for an Acquisition of Services are encouraged to use DAU's Acquisition Requirements Roadmap Tool (AART) to support the development of Performance Work Statements (PWS) or Statement of Objectives (SOO), Quality Assurance Surveillance Plans (QASP), and Performance Requirement Summaries (PRS). For service acquisitions valued at $1 billion or greater, USD(AT&L) mandates the use of the Services Acquisition Workshop (SAW) to develop the multifunctional acquisition requirements package. The SAW is a four-day workshop facilitated by DAU officials who guide the acquisition team through preparation of performance-based requirements using the AART.

PWS/SOO: This document should clearly define the performance objectives and standards that are expected of the contractor. The services are in terms of required results rather than how the work is to be accomplished. Define requirements to enable assessment of performance against measurable standards. Additionally, performance standards and incentives should be leveraged to encourage innovation and cost-effective methods of performing the service. A PWS template is located on the DITCO website. Instructions on how to write a PWS or SOO can be located on the DAU Services Acquisition Mall (SAM) website.

Requirements descriptions are considered to be performance work statements (PWS), or statements of objectives (SOO), when they include the following key aspects:

- A description of the expected output or outcomes or a statement expressing the performance characteristics
- A description of the environment in which the work will be performed
- Measurement criteria to compare actual versus expected performance.
- Procedures for rework or reduction in price if the item or service does not meet the performance standards

QASP: The QASP is the document that will be used to assess contractor performance under a services contract. The QASP identifies the measurable standards associated with the required tasks and the

specific inspections to be conducted. The QASP should be developed with customer feedback, with a focus on continuous improvement, and with a clear remedies and impacts for poor performance. Consider the cost and time to conduct surveillance and the value/importance of evaluating the contractor's performance on a certain task. Performance tasks with a lot of risk or mission criticality warrant a higher level of assessment than other tasks. For more information on how to write a QASP, visit the DAU SAM website.

Acceptable Quality Levels (AQLs): AQLs represent a deviation from a standard and can be used to establish a minimum number (or percentage) of acceptable outcomes that the government will accept. For example, an AQL might require a contractor to perform a task within one hour 95% of the time with an associated penalty if the 95% AQL isn't met. If used, AQLs should be realistic, measureable, and clearly communicated. AQLs may not be appropriate for Advisory and Assistance Services (A&AS) or Research and Development (R&D) services. AQLs should be incorporated in the QASP.

For additional information on requirements definition, reference Chapter IV, Section 1.

> **Key Questions:**
> - Does the PWS/SOO identify measureable performance objectives and outcomes?
> - Does the contract include performance incentives and disincentives?
> - Do the performance objectives align with industry best practices and standards?
> - Is the PWS/SOO constructed to allow the contractor(s) to deliver the service by following its own best practices?

9.1.3 Develop Cost Estimate

Based on the requirements identified for the service acquisition, the acquisition should develop and maintain a cost estimate. The level of detail will be commensurate with the size of the acquisition effort.

A detailed cost estimate containing a breakdown by cost element anticipated in the performance of the contract is required for all service acquisitions. The estimate should include direct costs such as labor, products, equipment, travel, and transportation; indirect costs such as labor overhead, material overhead, and general and administrative (G&A) expenses; and profit or fee (amount above costs incurred to remunerate the contractor for the risks involved in undertaking the contract). For a service acquisition, labor costs will most often be the most significant part of the estimate. The acquisition team should work with cost estimators and technical experts to identify the labor categories, skill levels, and the level of effort (work hours) required for each major task in the scope of work. The cost estimate will become the Independent Government Cost Estimate (IGCE) that will be used for the RFP documentation, as well as an important resource to evaluate the cost proposals during source selection.

For additional information on cost estimates, reference Chapter IV, Section 4.

113

> **Key Questions:**
> - Have rigorous cost estimates been conducted?
> - Are the services affordable within available funding?

9.1.4 Develop Service Level Agreements

SLAs are used to document and enforce contract terms and control the quality of performance. It is recommended that SLAs be used to cover, at a minimum, the following areas:

- Key contact information
- Hours of operation and location of services
- Escalation process
- Issue response and resolution times
- Performance guarantees
- Disaster recovery and business continuity
- Termination
- Data protection
- Cost

For additional information on SLAs, reference Chapter IV, Section 7.

> **Key Question:**
> - Have DISA SLAs been identified and incorporated into the RFP?

9.1.5 Refine Acquisition Strategy

This activity should build on the acquisition strategy developed in the initiation phase. The strategy should be updated to incorporate technical and market analysis and updated cost estimates. A well-defined PWS and QASP will guide the business strategy in determining the appropriate contract type, incentive arrangements, and type of acquisition supported by analysis of market research (e.g., existing DISA contract vehicle, other agency's contract vehicle, small business set-aside, Federal Supply Schedule, and commercial contracting). Acquisition Strategy examples can be found on the CAE website.

The Acquisition Plan is usually required for a new contract effort and must address the technical, business, management and other significant considerations to implement the approved acquisition strategy and must follow the format prescribed by FAR Part 7.105. In many cases, a combined Acquisition Strategy/Acquisition Plan can be used in lieu of separate documents. When using an existing contract vehicle, the acquisition team should check with the contracting office if an Acquisition Plan is required.

> **Key Questions:**
> - Is the strategy designed to maximize competition?
> - How will the contract type minimize risk to the government?

DISA IT Acquisition Guidebook

- Are existing contract vehicles available for the required services? If not, should DISA develop an enterprise contract vehicle for this service?
- Is the product/service a candidate for a DISA standard processing environment (e.g., RACE, FORGE.mil)?
- Are the resources requirements for the DISA standard processing environment and the associated migration activities adequately addressed in the acquisition strategy?
- If the service is not a candidate for the standard processing environment, has a waiver been obtained?
- Does the strategy plan specify the use of DISA standardized Service Operations tools (e.g. for pro-active monitoring, service-level compliance, and trouble-ticketing)?
- Does the strategy plan specify the operations functions that will support the capability (e.g. cognizant Service Desk, Technical Management, IT Operations Management, and Access Management teams) and how they will be resourced?
- Does the contract strategy address risk, incentives, data rights, and competition across the lifecycle?
- Is there a transition plan to deploy capabilities?
- Is there a plan to operate the capability in accordance with the DISA Service Operations Framework?
- Is there a realistic Integrated Master Schedule?
- Has the program identified and mitigated risks?
- Does the strategy require the service to comply with certification, accreditation, and IA requirements throughout the lifecycle?
- Does the strategy appropriately leverage contract type and objective incentives to motivate contractors to exceed minimum performance requirements?
- Have conflict-of-interest issues been addressed and eliminated or mitigation plans established?

9.1.6 Develop RFP Documents

The acquisition team will ensure that the procurement package is consistent with, and will result in, an executable service acquisition that is compliant with the acquisition strategy.

Contract recommendations (all recommendations may not be applicable in all IT service acquisitions but represent a good list of considerations that should be made in the contract negotiation process) include:

- List all additional and optional fees in the contract, such as additional storage fees and custom reports.
- The government should retain rights to COTS licensing and service data to enable transition to follow-on services and competition of sustainment or enhancement efforts.
- Include language that states who owns data during all of its lifecycle, including when data is transferred or exchanged (data in transit) and during storage (data at rest).
- Define what the contractor's responsibilities are in the event of a security breach or termination.

- Include confidentiality language relative to the DoD and the Federal Information Security Management Act (FISMA).
- Obtain detailed information about the contractor's security processes and procedures, including data flow diagrams.
- Ensure that the government has the right to audit the provider's facilities and documentation to verify that minimum security levels are in place and being enforced, including confirmation that government data is located where it should be and not being sent to a third party or being intermingled with other clients' data.
- Include a transition CLIN for both transition-in as well as transition-out at the end of the contract period.
- In Section L, include a cost template the vendors will complete. This will facilitate ease of analysis and comparison with the IGCE in the source selection.
- Include a liquidated damages clause to allow the government to collect dollars per calendar-day for delay when the contractor fails to deliver services on time.
- Include the option to extend services clause to allow the contract to be extended for up to 6 months in case there are issues with contract recompete and/or contract transition.
- Include the continuity of services clause to ensure that the contractor agrees to furnish phase-in training and exercise its best efforts and cooperation to effect an orderly and efficient transition to a successor.

For information on RFP documents, reference Chapter IV, Section 6.3.

Key Questions:
- Do the evaluation factors and subfactors enable the evaluation team to discriminate between offerors and select the contractor(s) best capable of providing the required outcomes?
- Is the source selection plan evaluation criteria tied to key program requirements?

9.1.7 Certify CCA

Clinger-Cohen Act (CCA) compliance by DISA CIO is required. For additional information on CCA compliance and certification, reference Chapter IV, Section 8.

9.1.8 Peer Review

All service contracts with an estimated value of $1 billion or more, including options (and any program designated special interest by AT&L), are required to complete a Defense Procurement and Acquisition Policy (DPAP) Peer Review. Additionally, for services that are below the $1 billion threshold, similar reviews should be conducted within DISA to ensure best practices in the acquisition of services. To align with DoD's Better Buying Power Initiative, strategic sourcing goals and metrics (such as utilization rates) should be included in the Peer Review Process to allow visibility at the department level.

Competitive procurements have three pre-award phases:
1. Prior to issuance of the solicitation

2. Prior to request for final proposal revisions
3. Prior to contract award

For non-competitive procurements, pre-award peer reviews shall be conducted at the pre- and post-business clearance phases.

Pre-award peer reviews assess the following elements:
1. The process was well understood by both government and industry.
2. Source selection was carried out in accordance with the Source Selection Plan and RFP.
3. The Source Selection Evaluation Board evaluation was clearly documented.
4. The Source Selection Advisory Council advisory panel recommendation was clearly documented.
5. The Source Selection Authority decision was clearly derived from the conduct of the source selection process.
6. All source selection documentation is consistent with the Section M evaluation criteria.
7. The business arrangement.

Post-award peer reviews shall assess the following elements:
1. Contract performance in terms of cost, schedule, and requirements.
2. Use of contracting mechanisms, including the use of competition, the contract structure and type, the definition of contract requirements, cost or pricing methods, the award and negotiation of task orders, and management and oversight mechanism.
3. The contractor's use, management, and oversight of subcontractors
4. The staffing of contract management and oversight function.
5. The extent of any pass-through charges and excessive pass-through charges by the contractor (as defined in DFARS 252.215-7004).

For contracts under which one contractor provides oversight for services performed by other contractors:
1. Extent of the DoD component's reliance on the contractor to perform acquisition functions closely associated with inherently governmental functions as defined in 10 U.S.C. 2383(b)(3).
2. The financial interest of any prime contractor performing acquisition functions described in paragraph 1 in any contract or subcontract with regard to which the contractor provided advice or recommendations to the agency.

For more information, visit the DPAP website for processes for completing the Peer Review process.

9.2 Decision Point 2

Decision Point 2 reviews the analysis and strategies for approval of the best approach to acquire the services (Selection Recommendation Document for Best Value Trade-Off or LPTA). It ensures that the strategy clearly identifies how it will obtain the desired service capability and how the program is

affordable to meet requirements within the available budget. The Decision Authority approves the release of the RFP.

The acquisition team should be prepared to answer the key questions identified above and provide the following information for Decision Point 2 approval:

Information Required at Decision Point 2:
- Acquisition Strategy (includes Analysis, Market Research, Technical Data Rights Strategy, Risk Assessment of potential technical, cost, schedule and performance risks)
- Independent Government Cost Estimate
- Acquisition Plan
- RFP, Contracting Documents (PWS/SOO, QASP, SSP, RFP, etc.)
- Service Level Agreements (when applicable)
- Clinger-Cohen Act Compliance

The acquisition team will prepare an Acquisition Decision Memorandum (ADM) and the Decision Authority will sign it. The ADM will capture the key decisions in the meeting, any action items for the acquisition team, and any guidance or deviations from policy and guidance for criteria for the source selection phase.

The source selection phase includes evaluating the proposals submitted and selecting the best value service solution for the government in accordance with the Source Selection Plan as well as planning and preparing to transition from an acquisition phase to the operate and sustain phase.

> **Best Practice Example**
>
> PEO-MA uses LPTA to compete engineering support services BPA to significantly speed up the source selection timeline for individual call orders.

9.3.1 Conduct Source Selection

The source selection phase includes evaluating the proposals submitted and selecting the service solution that best meets the government needs as well as planning and preparing to transition from an acquisition phase to the operate and sustain phase.

The source selection team will evaluate proposals in accordance with the evaluation factors stated in the RFP and Source Selection Plan to select the offeror whose proposal best meets the needs of the government. See DISA Acquisition Regulation Supplement (DARS) Subpart 15.3 for information on source selection responsibilities as well as additional guidance on the DITCO website.

Key questions that must be addressed at the Source Selection Decision include:
- Were proposals evaluated in accordance with the stated evaluation factors and subfactors in the RFP?
- Does the source selection decision support the selection of the best-value proposal consistent with the stated evaluation criteria?

9.3.2 Plan Transition Activities

Transition planning should be part of the acquisition process prior to source selection to ensure a smooth transition to the operations and support phase upon contract award. The Contracting Officer's Technical Representative (COTR) is critical to the transition process and should be involved throughout the acquisition process in anticipation of COTR duties upon contract award. This ensures an individual with knowledge and insight as to what is expected during contract performance.

Planning for an effective contract transition needs to begin long before the end of current contract period of performance. The necessary contract terms and conditions to enable effective contract transition need to be inserted into the contract and RFP at the time of original contract award.

A Contractor Transition-In plan should be requested as part of the RFP package. A recommended best practice is to include the Contract Transition-in Plan as part of the Contractor's Management or Technical Plan required under Section L of a solicitation. The government should also ensure that the Contractor Transition-in Plan is given appropriate weight as part of the Section M Evaluation factors. The government should carefully review the plan during the source selection evaluation to ensure the Offeror has provided a sound strategy to effectively phase-in their management team, assume day-to-day responsibilities, communicate with the incumbent contractor, and identify timelines with milestones associated with a schedule-based transition. For large complex services contracts such as those for enterprise resource planning or complex communication networks, the transition-in timeframe can require 90+ days. For smaller and more service-oriented or research and development requirements, 30–90 days is often considered a reasonable transition timeframe. A good Contract Transition-in Plan will provide several strategies for the new contractor to recruit new personnel and personnel currently employed by the incumbent, rather than relying on the retention of current personnel as the entire strategy.

Key Questions:
- Are transition activities in place if a service will transition from one contractor to another?
- Is the program preparing for a post-award conference to ensure mutual understanding of requirements and expectations, to define interface roles and responsibilities between government and contractor (to include interfacing with other contractors/FFRDCs), and to establish a foundation for a solid relationship and good communication with the contractor?

9.3.3 Certify CCA

Clinger-Cohen Act (CCA) compliance by DISA CIO is required. For additional information on CCA compliance and certification, reference Chapter IV, Section 8.

9.4 Source Selection Decision

The Source Selection Decision selects the proposal that meets the evaluation factors and performance requirements and provides the best value to the government. The Decision Authority approves contract award.

Information Required at Source Selection Decision:
- Source Selection Decision Document
- Integrated Checklist (if required)
- Authorization to Operate (ATO) (if required)
- Acquisition Lessons Learned and Best Practices
- Clinger-Cohen Act Compliance

9.5 Operate and Sustain

The objectives of this phase are to operate and support the capability for the user through the end of the intended lifecycle. Customer or user feedback and considerations for follow-on acquisitions are evaluated in this phase.

9.5.1 Conduct Transition Activities

To ensure success of the service, the transition of the program from acquisition to operation is critical. Sufficient resources from the acquisition team should be allocated to contract management to ensure effective and efficient performance throughout the life of the contract.

The program office should host a formal kick-off meeting or post-award conference with the contractor to establish a foundation for a solid relationship, good communication, and to achieve mutual understanding of contract requirements.

As part of the preparation for a new acquisition, it recommended that the acquisition team implement a Transition Planning Team that is responsible for monitoring the Contractor's Transition-In Plan. This transition team will participate in scheduled meetings with the contractor team to discuss transition topics to include facilities, GFE, contract deliverables, and contactor personnel. The team will review the contractor awardee's submitted plan versus the government provided items for completeness. Upon award start date, the contractor will work with the assigned government POC (Program Manager, Contracting Officer's Technical Representative, or designee) to ensure that actions are executed in accordance with the contractor's plan.

9.5.2 Manage Performance SLAs and Collect Metrics

SLAs establish baseline and minimum service levels and address provisioning and measurement of the network performance parameters. Performance in accordance with the SLAs should be collected, analyzed, and used to evaluate the value of the service provided to determine that minimum service levels are being met.

Appropriate metrics shall be collected to manage and evaluate the contractor's day-to-day performance in executing the services. The program shall collect and report information on service acquisitions to meet statutory and regulatory requirements. Required reporting information can be located on the CAE website.

SLAs must be applied consistently, maintained, and updated throughout the contract period of performance to ensure that performance objectives are achieved effectively. All SLAs supporting a particular effort should be managed collectively, and interdependencies should be identified and managed. To form a "meeting of the minds" between parties who may have competing agendas, SLAs should not be applied exclusively as a transactional and computer-generated communication of performance. SLAs should be applied as a mechanism for managing how the provider and government are expected to communicate and coordinate with one another. Measuring SLA conformance and reporting results are important aspects of the SLA process that help to ensure long-term consistency and results. In general, any major component of an SLA should be measurable, and a measurement methodology should be put in place prior to SLA implementation.

Because SLA administration and management can be resource-intensive, government organizations should review SLAs periodically to ensure that the stated performance requirements are still essential to achievement of overarching outcomes.

9.5.3 Obtain User Feedback

In addition to monitoring performance in accordance with the QASP, the program office should communicate regularly with all customers to ensure the service provided is meeting the requirements. Feedback from all customers should be formally documented and used to complete the required annual Contractor Performance Assessment Report (CPAR).

Chapter IV: Common Process Descriptions

As many of the processes are common across the IT acquisition models, this chapter captures DISA's approach to managing requirements, systems engineering, contracting, and many other acquisition elements. Each model in Chapter III identifies the key processes and model-unique aspects, and references this chapter for additional details. The processes identified in this chapter provide the foundation a team should implement for a sound acquisition, tailored based on size, risk, complexity, and related factors. An acquisition team isn't limited to their assigned staff; they should look across DISA to leverage the right expertise to develop and execute their program strategies.

For further information on acquisition processes, email the Acquisition Support Center or call 304-225-4150.

1   Requirements

In the initiation phase, the draft requirements are matured based on the alternatives analyzed, ROMs, understanding of cost drivers, market research, CONOPS, and continued collaboration with users and other stakeholders. Following Decision Point 1, when an IT acquisition model is selected, the requirements are further matured and either finalized and approved in a document or managed as a backlog in a database or related tool.

Programs using the JCIDS IT Box model via an IS ICD in the initiation phase will need to identify, develop, and submit subsequent requirements documents per their designated requirements oversight board. These may include a Requirements Definition Package (RDP), Capability Drop (CD), or alternative documents or databases that were agreed on.

Requirements definition is the most important and often the hardest step in this process. All members of the acquisition team should be strongly engaged in the requirements definition process to ensure a common understanding of CONOPS and programmatic impacts. All acquisitions of services shall be based on clear, performance-based requirements; include identifiable and measurable cost, schedule, and performance outcomes consistent with customer needs; and receive adequate planning and management to achieve those outcomes.

To drive affordability for DISA and its customers, it is critical that the team bound and define the requirements with sufficient cost/performance tradeoff analysis. Close collaboration with users, industry, systems engineers, and cost estimators is critical to understanding cost drivers, trade space, CONOPS impacts, and more.

DoD's traditional requirements processes and policies do not provide sufficient flexibility and speed to acquire IT. DISA—from an agency level to the individual program/project/service level—needs to manage requirements to support the unique demands of IT such as:

- More on dynamic requirements databases than in static documents.
- Encourages requirements changes during development to keep pace with technology and mission changes.
- Leverages industry standards and existing COTS/GOTS products to bound scope and performance standards and accelerate delivery of IT capabilities to warfighters.
- Governed by DISA's Enterprise Architecture and roadmaps to facilitate an integrated design.
- Integrates business process reengineering (BPR) of DoD processes to align with IT systems.
- Focuses on an integrated enterprise of products and services as opposed to program-centric solutions.
- Mission impact is the ultimate performance measure.

2   Systems Engineering

Systems engineering rigor shall provide the foundation of all acquisition programs within DISA. The acquisition team should reference the DISA Systems Engineering Reference Manual, DoD 5000, and the Defense Acquisition Guidebook for information on required systems engineering activities for each acquisition. Systems Engineering in DISA requires that programs develop artifacts to demonstrate that technical baselines are being maintained, managed, and controlled. The SE Reference Manual leverages industry best practices for implementing SE and process improvement approaches, including government directives and laws; USD(AT&L) policies; industry standards; Capability Maturity Model[®] Integration; ITIL, and the International Council on Systems Engineering (INCOSE).

Technical requirements should be based to the maximum extent practicable on open standards. Open Systems Architecture (OSA) is organized decomposition, using carefully defined execution boundaries, layered onto a framework of software and hardware shared services and a vibrant business model that facilitates competition. The acquisition team should refer to the Office of the Deputy Assistant Secretary of Defense (ODASD) Systems Engineering site, as well as the Open System Architecture Contract Guidebook for Program Managers for tools, strategies, and processes.

2.1   Develop Technical Baseline

The technical baseline is the state of IT from the current and desired state. The baseline manages and tracks the evolution of requirements, designs, configurations, development, integration, test, and other elements. It should serve as the foundation for the other programmatic elements (acquisition strategy, cost, test, etc.). As the program progresses through the acquisition lifecycle, the technical baseline will mature with increasing rigor, number of data sources, and fidelity of details.

The core of a technical baseline (see Table 5) is primarily the description, design, and decomposition of the system's hardware, software, and integration.

Table 5. Technical Baseline Core

Core Elements of a Technical Baseline	Related Elements to Align/Integrate
System decomposition of subsystems, hardware and software components, developments, and COTS/GOTS	DISA Enterprise Architecture
Integration at multiple levels	System dependencies and interfaces
Technical designs	Performance standards, models, and analysis
Test plans and results	CONOPS and Requirements including Key Performance Parameters (KPPs) if applicable
Technology strategy: maturity, insertion, and refresh	Cost models and estimates and program/portfolio budgets
Allocation of capabilities across increments, releases, or spirals	Acquisition Strategies and schedules
Pilots and prototypes	Enterprise Roadmaps
Risk summary	Development, operations, maintenance, and sustainment strategies
Technical platforms or infrastructure	Legacy systems, components, baselines and the transition strategies
Information Assurance	

Beyond the core elements, the technical baseline should include a system/functional description, key performance parameters, enterprise architectures, interfaces, standards, technology maturity, and evolution strategy. It may also provide technical context such as legacy capability migration, reuse, and operating environment, and disposal. Performance models and analyses could also be included as part of the technical baseline. Information assurance, service management, testing, and other critical engineering constraints need to be translated into development activities that will be performed. The comprehensive technical baseline should be developed by the acquisition team independent of the prime contractor's designs. This provides the government with a detailed reference design to use as the basis for cost estimates, risk analysis, requirements prioritization, tradeoff studies, and negotiations with the contractor.

The technical baseline should be aligned with the DISA Enterprise Architecture and reviewed by the Chief Engineers Panel (CEP) to ensure compliance. This includes having a thorough understanding of the requirements, technologies, interfaces, standards, reuse opportunities, risks, test criteria, and other elements of the program. The CEP will issue an Engineering Decision Memorandum (EDM) to confirm compliance. As the program matures through the acquisition lifecycle, continual collaboration with the CEP is required to ensure architecture alignment. For more information DISA's Enterprise Architecture, visit the CEP website.

The data sources for the technical baseline may be found in the following documents:

DISA IT Acquisition Guidebook

- IT Inventory
- CONOPS
- Service Operations Annex (for Enterprise Services)
- Technology Development Strategy
- Requirements Documents or Databases
- Acquisition Strategy
- System Engineering Plan
- Interface Control Documents
- Life Cycle Sustainment Plan
- Information Support Plan
- Cost Analysis Requirements Description (MAIS programs)
- WBS and WBS dictionary
- Acquisition Program Baseline
- DISA Enterprise Architecture and related products

The ability to affect lifecycle cost is maximized early in a program and diminishes rapidly as solution decisions are made. To design affordability into programs, acquisition team leaders should make integrated cost and capability decisions throughout the program, beginning as early as possible. To enable that, the technical baseline should be aligned with a cost baseline that includes cost models and cost estimates. They should also be aligned with the program schedules to understand the schedule impacts and dependencies of each element.

This collaborative, integrated, rigorous effort is critical to delivering required IT capabilities in a dynamic technical, budget, and operational environment.

2.2 Systems Engineering Tradeoffs

Once the underlying baselines have been developed and integrated, the team can assess the impact of each element on cost, schedule, technical performance, and risk. These tradeoffs help scope and design the program into an affordable solution. It can also support DISA's pricing strategies for enterprise services. This requires a multi-disciplinary team to understand the technical aspects as well as the full programmatic impacts and trade space.

Trade studies can be done early with the alternatives analysis to explore options for designs, strategies, and lifecycle evolution and support. They can be conducted in later phases to examine the optimal deployment,

Key Considerations

If the program's budget were cut by 10%, 25%, or 50%, what would be the impact on requirements, capabilities, schedules, or technical performance? What capabilities require a lengthy development timeline that needs to be planned within the release size and frequency? If the last 10% of technical performance cost 25% or more of the program's budget, would the requirements sponsor support de-scoping or deferring that capability?

can focus on a high-priority or high-risk technical performance requirement as part of a larger tradeoff analysis.

The acquisition team should have a clear understanding of the priorities and constraints to drive the analysis. This could include delivering a set of capabilities within a certain budget, price point, or schedule. It could be to address a technical risk or to maximize technical performance. The mission and operational environment must be clearly understood with active collaboration with warfighters on CONOPS, gaps, and cost/schedule/performance tradeoffs. Similarly the trade space within the enterprise architecture needs to be understood to see if changes to standards, interfaces, and connected systems are viable variables.

Tradeoffs may be in the system functions, features, or performance. This includes the system capabilities, the ways the capabilities are performed, and the quantitative measures. The acquisition and sustainment strategy tradeoffs are mostly the acquisition models the program would follow. Is it better to develop it new, integrate COTS/GOTS products and/or acquire the capability or supporting operations and maintenance via a service?

The team should have clearly defined constraints, assumptions, evaluation criteria, and weights to guide them through this analysis. The amount of rigor of this analysis will depend on the size, scope, and complexity of the program. The analysis and underlying data should be saved so the team can revisit it in the future to provide additional information, constraints, risks, and alternatives to have a current appreciation of options. Sharing the analysis across DISA enables reuse, integration, and minimizes duplication when other programs/initiatives explore a similar effort.

The tradeoff analysis should be coordinated with key stakeholders to validate the analysis, results, and impacts. A common understanding will best support decisions by those with the proper authority.

2.3 Technical Reviews

DISA acquisitions will include a tailored series of technical reviews throughout the lifecycle to evaluate significant achievements and assess technical maturity and risk. MAIS programs will use most of the eleven technical reviews outlined in the Defense Acquisition Guidebook, whereas most DISA programs will focus on four reviews that best apply to IT acquisitions. The use of and amount of rigor of each review will vary based on the program, the acquisition model being used, and the systems engineering plan.

- **Alternative Systems Review (ASR)**—Conducted in the initiation phase at the end of an alternatives analysis, the ASR focuses technical efforts on requirements analysis to support a dialogue among the acquisition team and end users.
- **System Requirements Review (SRR)**—Conducted after requirements have been documented and finalized, the SRR focuses on validating requirements and ensuring an open dialogue among the acquisition team, end users, requirements community, and operations support.

126

- **Design Review (DR)** – To ensure that the system design and can meet the stated performance requirements within cost (budget), schedule, risk, and other constraints.
- **Test Readiness Review (TRR)**—`The TRR assesses the contractor's readiness for testing configuration items, including hardware and software, with respect to the test objectives, procedures, resources, and testing coordination; and ensures that the subsystem or system under review is ready to proceed into formal test.

For more information on Technical Reviews at DISA, reference the DISA Systems Engineering Reference Manual.

3 Acquisition Strategy

The Acquisition Strategy is the key effort that pulls together all the acquisition elements into a concise document. It must outline the program's structure, schedule, market research, contracting strategy, test and evaluation strategy, budget and cost analysis summary, risks and mitigations, integration strategy, acquisition team processes (e.g., systems engineering technical reviews), initial sustainment strategy, service operations approach, and other elements. It will evolve over time with increased fidelity as the program progresses through its acquisition lifecycle. The size and level of detail will be commensurate with the size and complexity of the acquisition. A guide/template on DISA Acquisition Strategies can be found on the CAE website.

Some elements of the strategy may be briefly summarized in the acquisition strategy, with the details captured in a separate document like a Systems Engineering Plan, Test and Evaluation Management Plan, or Acquisition Plan. The acquisition leader can make the decision to summarize these activities in the acquisition strategy or use separate documentation. Although these documents will be reviewed and approved by the appropriate Decision Authority, *they are primarily for the acquisition team to use to plan, develop, and execute their strategies.*

The acquisition strategy document is intended to be a streamlined document that consolidates many of the required DoD 5000 documents. Reference Appendix C for a list of required DoD 5000 documentation and the elements that have been consolidated into the acquisition strategy document.

The acquisition strategy should include the following information:

- Requirements
- Program considerations (e.g., security, interoperability, IA, logistics, CONOPS, service management)
- Acquisition program structure
- Acquisition and contracting approach
- Program management approach
- Risk management strategy
- Lifecycle cost summary
- Funding strategy

- Resource management
- Acquisition schedule
- Technical analysis results
- Market research strategy and results
- Pilot/prototyping activities and results
- Information support plan
- Technical data rights strategy
- Systems engineering strategy
- Architecture views
- Test and evaluation strategy
- Service operations approach
- Lifecycle sustainment strategy

A few of the key acquisition documents that will be consolidated into the Acquisition Strategy are briefly described as follows:

Systems Engineering Plan (SEP): This document captures the systems engineering approach that guides the program's technical activities. It documents technical risks, processes, resources, metrics, products, and schedules. It is a living document that should be kept current throughout the program lifecycle and aligned to related documents like the Acquisition Strategy. The SEP details are tailored to the size, complexity, scope, and lifecycle support of the acquisition. Additional guidance is located in the DISA Systems Engineering Reference Manual, Version 6.3, Dec 2011, the DASD/SE Policy website (SEP Guide), and the Defense Acquisition Guidebook Chapter 4.1.2.

Test & Evaluation Strategy: This document describes the test and evaluation processes, resources, risks, tools, schedules, organizations, platforms, and related elements. They are tailored to the size, complexity, scope, and life-cycle support of the acquisition. It is a living document that should be kept current throughout the program lifecycle and aligned to related documents like the Acquisition Strategy and SEP. DISA T&E Strategy template/guide can be found on the DISA Testing Office website. Additional T&E guidance is located on the DAU ACQuipedia and the Defense Acquisition Guidebook Chapter 9.

Lifecycle Sustainment Plan (LCSP): IT products and services must integrate sustainment considerations in the early stages of the program and throughout design, development, testing, deployment, and sustainment. Operations and sustainment costs are often the largest component of a program's lifecycle costs. The LCSP describes the approach and resources necessary to develop and integrate sustainment requirements throughout the lifecycle and should align to related documents above. Additional guidance on lifecycle sustainment can be found on the DAU's ACQuipedia and Defense Acquisition Guidebook Chapter 5.1.

Acquisition Program Baseline (APB): APBs capture a program's cost, schedule, and performance objective and threshold values. They are required for all ACAT programs. Non-ACAT programs,

128

projects, or services must capture their cost, schedule, and performance baselines in their Acquisition Strategy or Program Execution Plan, or they can create an APB. Additional APB guidance is located in the Defense Acquisition Guidebook, Chapter 10.9.

4   Cost Estimating

Each program or project must develop and maintain a lifecycle cost estimate. The level of detail will be commensurate with the size of the program. At a minimum, the cost estimate should include a work breakdown structure, ground rules and assumptions, and a basis of estimate, and it should be based on a technical baseline. For MAIS and MDAP programs the WBS must adhere to the WBS structure provided in the MID STD 881C directive. The DISA CFE support team will provide cost support guidance and will identify the level of cost estimate rigor required for all acquisitions. For complex cost estimates, it is recommended that the acquisition team bring in cost estimating support, especially in cases when the acquisition team will also need to develop a DISA pricing model for DISA-provided fee- for-services (e.g., Enterprise Services). Please note that for those programs designation ACAT III and above, a formal Independent Cost Estimate (ICE) will be required.

It is important to delineate the costs for the government programmatics (e.g., acquisition team, requirements, contracting, and architecture) as well as IA/security compliance, from the costs to develop, integrate, test, deploy, and operate the IT capabilities. Cost information from historical data and analogous programs/projects can be used to develop a basis of estimate. The estimate should be developed using a standardized process such as the one developed and implemented by GAO, depicted in Figure 15.

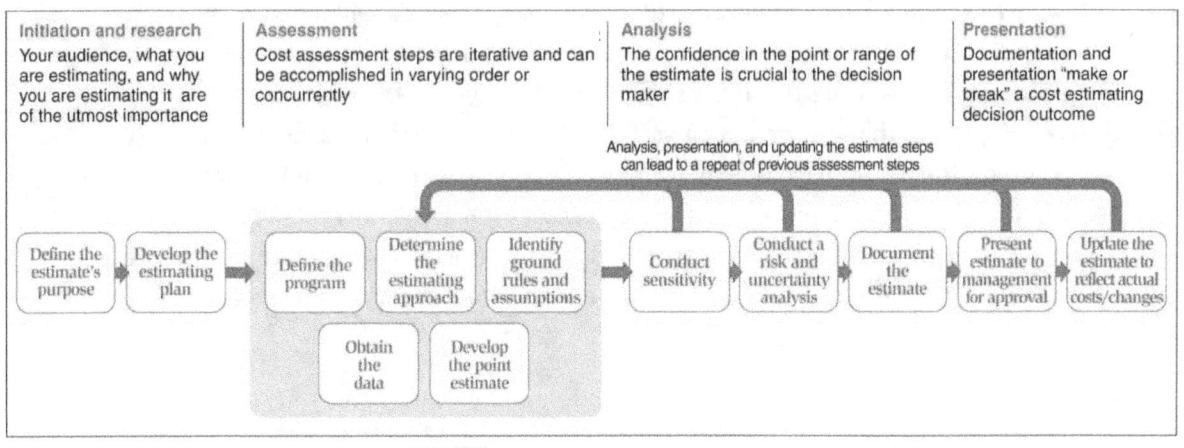

Source: GAO.

Figure 15 GAO Standardized Process Model

Things to consider when developing a cost estimate include:

- What are the hardware and software components required for the system?
- Do any of the components require custom develop or is everything off-the-shelf?
- Will special integration software be needed to ensure compatibility between the components?

- Will building modifications (e.g., flooring, additional drops, etc.) be required to accommodate the new and/or modified hardware)?
- Will specialized labor be required to develop and/or maintain the system?
- Can any economies of scale be realized through bundling?
- Can any existing infrastructure or technologies be leveraged?
- Are costs for pre-planned program initiatives (P3I) captured?
- Are costs for data transfers from legacy systems captured?
- Have costs for RACE and Cloud been considered?
- Conducting Risk and Uncertainty Analysis
  - Determine and discuss with technical experts the level of cost, schedule, and technical risk associated with each WBS element
  - Analyze each risk for its severity and probability
  - Develop minimum, most likely, and maximum ranges for each risk element
  - Determine the type of risk distributions and reason for their use
  - Ensure that the risks are correlated
  - Use an acceptable statistical analysis method (e.g. Monte Carlo simulation) to develop a confidence interval around the point estimate
  - Identify the confidence level of the point estimate
  - Determine the risk-adjusted cost estimate

The cost estimate should be tightly coupled with the technical baseline to ensure a clear understanding of the cost drivers and cost/performance trade space, and to enable scenario planning. The cost estimate should be revisited at each major milestone/decision point, and if designated ACAT III or above, the program will require the estimate to be updated annually; however, at a minimum, within each phase of the acquisition, the acquisition team should work closely with the engineers to synchronize the cost estimate with the current technical baseline. Performing this activity on a continuous basis will allow the program to compare costs to the available budget to determine program/project affordability. The personnel performing the cost estimating function should work closely and regularly with the acquisition team to further enable these activities. Program managers are required to regularly identify means to reduce program costs throughout the program lifecycle to deliver the best value to the defense enterprise.

Pricing information to use for cost estimates can be located through several sources, including:

- Supplier catalogs
- Electronic Internet search engines (Yahoo, Google, All the Web, and Ask.com, etc.)
- Government "electronic malls"
- Data readily available from market research (comparative information regarding competitors and the competitive environment)
- Data available from government purchasing/engineering activities (purchase history, engineering estimates, etc.)

- Analogies—comparative pricing information for similar items
- Parametric analyses (rough yardstick correlation based on thrust, range, processing speed, weight, or other technical factors or item characteristics)
- Advice from government pricing and audit personnel
- Operations stakeholders to identify operational costs
- Company historical records
- Industry association databases

Cost estimates should include the entire life of a program through operations and sustainment and disposal if applicable. "Should cost" and "will cost" targets, as defined in the Better Buying Power, will be established and used to support contract negotiations and profit incentive structures, as well as being used as a management tool.

In this fiscal environment, it is the responsibility of every program and portfolio manager to continually assess and implement opportunities for cost efficiencies. This is especially important in an operations and sustainment phase because those costs typically are the majority of total life cycle costs. Efficiency assessments and efficiency projects should be part of the program/portfolio plan. Efficiency assessments include analyzing cost drivers, evaluating cost savings opportunities, evaluating new technology for potential cost savings, and assessing acquisition strategy alternatives for reduced cost. Efficiency opportunities to consider are very broad, the following are just a few to consider;

The factors identified in OSD(AT&L) Better Buying Power
- Increased automation
- Increase competition, with contract incentives to include efficiency
- Economies of scale through partnerships
- Open/Agile architecture with defined standards for easier technology/capability insertion
- Consolidation of support services
- Improved user support tools
- Streamlined operational processes to lower labor requirements
- Changing future government/contractor roles responsibilities (buy as a service vs product)

Once efficiency opportunities are decided on, they should be managed as a project through implementation (at the point it becomes part of the normal sustainment activities) and savings should be tracked.

For more information on cost estimates:

- DAG Chapter 3.7 on the Principles for Lifecycle Cost Estimates
- GAO Cost Estimating and Assessment Guide
- DoD Standard Practice, Work Breakdown Structures for Defense Materiel Items

5 Business Process Reengineering

Business Process Reengineering (BPR) is redesigning the way work is conducted to better support the organization's mission and reduce costs. As information systems and networks become more sophisticated and widespread, it is critical to ensure that these systems are designed for optimum effectiveness and efficiency. The intent of BPR in this model is to redesign DISA business processes, to the maximum extent possible, to conform to the best practice business rules inherent in the COTS product. Adopt the COTS/GOTS solution as is "out-of-the-box" rather than adapting it to accommodate existing systems and processes.

For COTS acquisitions, additional BPR is conducted after program initiation, to reengineer an organization's retained processes to match available COTS processes.

An effective BPR team should be comprised of:

- Individuals who understand reengineering and its impacts on the organization
- Process subject matter experts from the organization
- Cross-functional resources from impacted areas
- Systems integrator resources with expert knowledge of the processes inherent in the software

6 Contracting

The acquisition team is encouraged to use performance-based contracts to the maximum extent possible. The maximum use of existing contract vehicles is recommended for all DISA acquisitions, especially DISA enterprise contract vehicles such as ENCORE II. More information on DISA enterprise vehicles can be located on the DITCO website.

DISA programs are encouraged to adopt an open systems architecture concept in accordance with AT&L Better Buying Power initiative. The acquisition team should refer to the Open Systems Architecture Contract Guidebook for Program Managers for additional information.

6.1 Industry Engagement

Industry engagement can provide insight into technology trends, emerging capabilities, risks, and opportunities. DISA regularly shares its vision, challenges, and trends, but the agency can go further to share initial strategies on capabilities that it plans to acquire (with appropriate contracting officer guidance). Companies can provide valuable feedback on these strategies, propose recommendations, and convey their interest in pursuing that work. Acquisition teams can coordinate with industry early in the design phase using Requests for Information, sources sought synopsis, and public forums to assist developing the acquisition strategy. Though DISA is an enterprise solution provider to the Department of Defense, it is through strategic partnerships with industry that DISA can succeed in its mission. Although some aspects of strategy need to be close hold for obvious reasons, the more can be shared with industry, the better informed DISA will be to deliver effective and efficient capabilities to the warfighter.

The acquisition team can use the information contained in the Better Buying Power "Myth-Busting" memorandums for information on industry outreach practices.

6.2 Market Research

Market research needs to be conducted before developing new specifications for procurement and before soliciting bids or proposals for a contract in excess of the simplified acquisition threshold. Additionally, acquisition personnel must create acquisition strategies and plans that facilitate the introduction or incorporation of evolving commercial items into defense systems. As part of such an integrated market research effort, the government should also communicate early and often with the commercial sector.

Representatives from all disciplines (e.g., program, contracting, logistics, budget and small business)

> **Best Practice Recommendation**
>
> Issue a Request for Information (RFI) on www.FedBizOpps.gov to identify that DISA is exploring acquiring a particular IT capability.. The RFI could solicit responses from companies that may be interested in bidding, identify related programs or technologies, and request suggestions from industry to help shape the acquisition strategy. Coordinate with PLD for further information on RFIs in DISA.
>
> The team can also leverage sites like http://www.defenseinnovationmarketplace. mil to connect with industry. This site can be used to share DISA priorities and capability needs and research the industry capabilities and IR&D projects.

need to be included early in the process. Information gathered during market research should be used to refine the requirements to maximize the benefit of competitive market forces. To provide input to the team for the acquisition strategy/plan, contracting personnel gather information on customary contract terms and conditions, representative incentive provisions, and pricing practices.

Some market research techniques include:

- Contacting knowledgeable individuals in Government and industry regarding market capabilities.
- Reviewing results of recent market research reports covering similar items.
- Publishing formal requests for information.
- Querying Internet information sources (Vendor/Industry site).
- Gathering market information on specific products and potential suppliers.
- Gathering market pricing and technical information from commercial or government sources.
- Gathering market information on industry practices, supply and demand trends, and other relevant factors.
- Obtaining source lists from other agencies and professional associations.
- Reviewing industry catalogs and product literature.
- Conducting interchange meetings or holding pre-solicitation conferences and other government-industry interchanges

- Visiting contractors; attending industry and trade shows.
- Gathering information from market or trade journals and magazine.

For the acquisition of a commercial item, market research should look at:

Available Sources
- What and how many are available?
- What is/are the market and corporate strategies in industry?
- What are the technical strengths and weaknesses of the commercial items?
- What kind of support capabilities does the product/service offer?
- What are the commercial data rights of the product/service?

Available Supplies and Services
- Typical commercial customizing or tailoring
- Potential cost of modifying the item to meet current needs
- Salient characteristics
- Prices
- Tradeoffs
- Reliability, history, and past performance

Industry Practices and Trends
- Industry specifications and standards
- Customary terms and conditions, such as discounts and warranties
- Relevant laws and regulations
- Production and delivery lead times
- Forecast product/technology changes
- Trends in market prices
- Trends in supply/demand
- Factors that affect market prices

Market research must continue throughout the entire acquisition process, not only because it is required by statute, but also, more important, because it gathers the data needed for making smart acquisition decisions.

The acquisition team will conduct in-depth market research to address the business and technical considerations of the requirements. This includes identifying existing contracts (internal and external to the agency) via the Government wide database of contracts (Interagency Contract Directory). The database includes Government-Wide Acquisition Contracts, Multi-Agency Contracts, Indefinite Delivery Contracts, Federal Supply Schedules, Basic Ordering Agreements, and Blanket Purchase Agreements. The team is also encouraged to engage with industry for additional market research. Once the market

research is complete, the team analyzes and documents the findings and recommendations in the acquisition strategy. Additional information on market research can be located on the DAU Services Acquisition Mall website as well as the DITCO website.

6.3 Develop RFP Documents

SOW/PWS/SOO: This document should clearly define the performance objectives and standards that are expected of the contractor. The contract requirements should be expressed in terms of required results rather than how the work is to be accomplished. Requirements should be defined to enable assessment of performance against measurable standards. Additionally, performance standards and incentives should be leveraged to encourage innovation and cost effective methods of performance. DISA PWS templates are located on the DITCO website. Instructions on how to write a PWS or SOO can be located on the DAU Services Acquisition Mall (SAM) website.

Requirements descriptions are considered to be performance work statements (PWSs), or statements of objectives (SOOs), when they include the following key aspects:

- A description of the expected output or outcomes or a statement expressing the performance characteristics
- A description of the environment in which the work will be performed
- Measurement criteria to compare actual versus expected performance
- Procedures for rework or reduction in price if the item or service does not meet the performance standards

If using a SOO, the RFP should request that the offerors develop a PWS and propose a QASP with proposed SLAs. A well-defined PWS and QASP will guide the business strategy in determining the appropriate contract type, incentive arrangements, and type of acquisition supported by analysis of market research (e.g., existing DISA contract vehicle, other agency's contract vehicle, small business set-aside, Federal Supply Schedule, commercial contracting).

Quality Assurance Surveillance Plan: The QASP document is used to assess contractor performance under a services contract. The QASP identifies the measurable standards associated with the required tasks and the specific inspections to be conducted. The QASP should be developed with customer feedback, with a focus on continuous improvement, and with a clear remedies and impacts for poor performance. Consider the cost and time to conduct surveillance and the value/importance of evaluating the contractor's performance on a certain task. Performance tasks with a lot of risk or mission criticality warrant a higher level of assessment than other tasks. For more information on how to write a QASP, visit the DAU SAM website.

Acquisition Plan: The Acquisition Plan is usually required for a new contract effort and must address the technical, business, management and other significant considerations to implement the approved Acquisition Strategy and must follow the format prescribed by FAR Part 7.105. In many cases, a

135

combined Acquisition Strategy/Acquisition Plan can be used in lieu of separate documents. When using an existing contract vehicle, the acquisition team should check with the contracting office if an Acquisition Plan is required.

Independent Government Cost Estimate (IGCE): The IGCE is the government's estimate of the resources and projected cost of the resources a contractor will incur in the performance of a contract. These costs include direct costs such as labor, products, equipment, travel, and transportation; indirect costs such as labor overhead, material overhead, and general and administrative (G&A) expenses; and profit or fee (amount above costs incurred to remunerate the contractor for the risks involved in undertaking the contract). The IGCE should include only those elements applicable to and developed from the SOO/SOW/PWS or description of the supplies, services, or construction to be acquired. An IGCE is required for every procurement action in excess of the simplified acquisition threshold at FAR 2.101. For more information on developing an IGCE, reference the DoD COR Handbook.

Source Selection Plan: The source selection plan is required for any competitive acquisition and identifies the source selection team, the evaluation factors from the RFP, and the specific procedures that will be used to evaluate contractor proposals as Lowest Price Technically Acceptable (LPTA) or Best-Value Trade-Off. The document also serves as an internal agreement and guide for the evaluation team on the conduct of the entire source selection from proposal evaluation,

> **Best Practice Example**
>
> PEO-MA uses LPTA to compete engineering support services BPA to significantly speed up the source selection timeline for individual call orders.

through the cost/price/technical tradeoff, award decision, and debriefing. Source selection factors and subfactors should be developed to allow for meaningful discrimination among offeror(s). Additional information and samples are available on the DITCO website.

Request for Proposal: The RFP package is developed with the Contracting Office. The RFP, at a minimum, will include the PWS/SOO, Contract Line Items, terms and conditions, and proposal instructions and evaluation criteria. All of the parts of the solicitation must work together to communicate the government's requirements. The solicitation provides all the information the offeror needs to understand what is being bought, how it is being bought, and how the source will be selected. Issuing a draft RFP is a method to solicit industry feedback on the requirements and proposed business strategy. It also provides the government with insight into the number of contractors interested in the acquisition. The acquisition team should include an adequate amount of time in the schedule to conduct this activity. The documents required for a complete RFP package are located on the DITCO website.

7 Service Level Agreements

If the acquired service is to be provided as a DISA service as part of DISA's Service Catalog, Service Level Agreements (SLAs) are necessary to establish performance thresholds for the service and to ensure quality of service, interoperability, and availability of network management data exchanged between

systems and with any authorized user IAW DoDI 8410.03, Network Management policy, section 4 of Enclosure 3. Operational performance of the services defined in the SLA will be monitored, measured, and reported against the commitments defined in the agreement.

Any solid SLA should contain specific, measurable and enforceable terms and conditions that the service provider must adhere to for each component of the service provided. The specific performance requirements of the SLA should be expressed in terms of end-user experience, rather than back-end performance. Also, if applicable, graduated levels of performance with varying prices should be outlined in the SLA. If the provider fails to meet an obligation under the SLA, the SLA must have the "teeth" to help mitigate such failure from happening again. The "teeth" for SLAs are the specific remedies that apply when the provider's obligations are not met. The penalties should be consistent with the severity and priority levels assigned. The remedies usually take the form of monetary damages that are pre-agreed between the parties for specific failures and/or credits for future services.

An SLA is used to document and enforce added terms (performance metrics and measures) intended to control the quality of performance of the provider's service. SLAs are cited as examples of performance controls, and as means of implementing performance incentives, in the use of performance-based services. Here are a few tips on how to construct a good SLA:

- The service being controlled must be measurable on objective levels of some kind, by formulas that both sides agree will be used for performance control purposes. Thus the definition of the term "service level."
- Procedures for collecting the data to use to compute service levels must be specified to ensure that the data is relevant and sufficient for measurement purposes.
- If periods of time are applicable in the use of a given measure, the procedures related to how such time periods will be determined and recorded must also be specified.
- Performance measures are agreed on at the beginning of a period of performance and then not changed during the period of performance except by mutual agreement.
- As a general check for determining that the rules are relevant and sufficient, the rules and criteria, plus the collected data for a given period, are provided to a technically competent unbiased external third party. The external party should be able to interpret the data, apply the rules and criteria, and reach the same conclusions that the parties to the agreement would.
- To ensure that service management focus is placed on delivering service to end-users, the service-level metrics should measure the end-user experience/customer satisfaction which should be tracked through surveys, etc
- Understand business objectives, focusing on partnership between IT and business.
- Baseline what is being delivered today and what can be measured.
- Revisit the SLA on a periodic basis or when business needs change. They should be updated periodically to reflect incremental improvements due to technology changes and ongoing process/procedural improvements.

Metrics are an integral part of a well-defined SLA. They are included to monitor the performance of services specified within an SLA. Metrics are also necessary for enforcing an SLA because they help in detecting violations of promised performance levels and in determining consequential actions associated with the violations. A majority of metrics included in an SLA can be characterized as "direct metrics." Direct metrics are either measured or retrieved directly from a managed resource. The other type of metric included in an SLA is called a "composite metrics" which is a mathematical composition of direct metrics and therefore it is computed and not measured.

Since metrics are the key ingredients of an SLA, it is essential that they should be rigorously defined. From a best practices perspective, a metric definition should minimally include the following characteristics:

- Rigorous measurement definition that enables objective measurement of the metric
- Calculations needed to produce the metric from measurements
- Support for customer requirements including compliance issues
- Focus on effectiveness and efficiency of the process being measured
- Support for meaningful trend or statistical analysis
- Adherence to appropriate industry standards
- Clear statement of assumptions being applied
- Frequency of measurement
- Reporting requirements
- Clear statement of the end result expected which could either be a threshold or a range of values that satisfy the expected level of performance
- Responsibilities for monitoring and enforcement
- Incentives and penalties aligned to expected performance

For more information on how to write SLAs, reference the CISCO Service Level Management: Best Practices White Paper, Best Practices for Service-Level Management by Forrester Research, and SLA Template.

8   Clinger-Cohen Act

All DISA programs containing IT, regardless of ACAT or other designation, must be confirmed for Clinger-Cohen Act (CCA) compliance prior to all milestones, decision points, and major contract awards. Per DISA Instruction 630-225-9, the DISA CIO will certify to the DoD CIO DISA MDAP or MAIS programs are in compliance with CCA. The acquisition team lead will confirm to the DISA CIO compliance with CCA for any non-MDAP or MAIS program below $5 million in all years or $1 million in any fiscal year. These programs may be subject to an audit by the CIO to verify CCA compliance.

CCA compliance and reporting applies to the acquisition, management, operation, and closure of all IT investments, as well as to all programs that acquire IT. The acquisition team lead will use the DISA CCA Compliance Checklist during the initiation phase and throughout the lifecycle as appropriate. For

additional information on CCA Certification, visit the Defense Acquisition Guidebook (Chapter 7.8) and DISA Instruction 630-225-9.

9   Continual Technology Development (Pilots, Prototypes)

The acquisition team should continue piloting/prototyping activities conducted in the early phases. Given the rapid pace of change in information technology, DISA must continue to be active in the development and adoption of the leading technologies. Traditional acquisition policies focus technology development on maturing the technology for the next increment of work. In DISA acquisition, the goal is to have a *continual environment for technology development* where we can continue to prototype, pilot, mature, integrate, and demonstrate the leading technologies available in the government and commercial sectors. This development environment will ensure that mature technologies are available for inclusion in the next increment, release, or project. This environment may be developed at a portfolio level to feed multiple smaller programs. Collaboration with R&D communities from DARPA, IARPA, government labs, test ranges, government and industry technology groups, FFRDCs, and the commercial sector are recommended. Additionally, forums for businesses (particularly small businesses) to demonstrate their capabilities or address challenges DISA has posed to the community would further support this continual technology development environment. The team should consider use of DISA's Rapid Access Computing Environment (RACE) and milCloud to support continual technology development. These tools enable rapid transition from development, to test and production environments.

Pilots are an effective risk reduction technique to demonstrate or integrate a subset of capabilities or user groups before a full deployment of capabilities to the enterprise. This gives the team performance results in an operational environment for comparison against requirements and alternatives. Given the rapid pace of change in IT (often 18–24 months), the scope and timelines for pilots must factor in the technologies useful lifespan. Pilots should often be scoped to less than a year, often with a cost of under $1 million based on the size of the total program. Timelines for contracting, integration, testing, and certification must be streamlined to support these aggressive timelines.

When exploring the use and scope of a pilot, the acquisition team should consider these factors:

- What is the intent of the pilot? Risk reduction?
- If these capabilities are in use today in the DoD or commercial environment, could they provide valuable insight to complement or supplement pilots?
- What metrics, feedback, or performance measurements do you plan to review from the pilots?
- What is the cost and likely schedule for pilots and how do they feed into the larger program?
- What are the measures of success for the pilots?

For more information, reference the Carnegie Mellon Software Engineering Institute presentation on Conducting Effective Pilot Studies.

139

10 Testing

Risk assessments are performed to determine appropriate level(s) of test, and/or to tailor testing to focus on the program's highest risk areas. Risk assessments are generally based upon two factors: 1) Likelihood of a Failure (LoF) occurring, and 2) impact if the failure occurs. Risk areas are dependent upon the program, but generally cover the areas of technology, integration, operational profile, management, and Information Assurance. A good risk assessment will examine the likelihood of failure in each of these areas, and assess the resulting impact to the mission, the network, interfacing and/or other dependent systems/services, security, and to customer/user satisfaction. The output of the risk assessment is used to design a testing regimen to mitigate the risks.

Developmental Test and Evaluation (DT&E) is performed to verify that the system under test meets all technical requirements. DT&E should be used to verify the status of technical progress on Pilot and Prototype systems and to certify the readiness for Initial Operational testing. DT&E in a software environment is usually performed in a mode to collect sufficient data to validate the performance against the technical requirements. Developmental testing is used to isolate and fix defects in a system prior to full scale production or release.

Operational Test and Evaluation (OT&E) is primarily used to inform the specific decision to place a product into operational use, regardless of the acquisition model employed. OT&E determines the operational effectiveness, suitability, interoperability, and security of the program or service in its intended operational environment. In ITIL terms, effectiveness and interoperability are considered utility, and suitability and security are considered Warranty. The level of OT&E required depends upon the output of the risk assessment, and the scope of dedicated/specific OT&E events depends upon how well the overall test strategy integrates the events across the entire testing regimen. The best practice is to develop the program's operational evaluation strategy early in the life cycle. The evaluation strategy clearly defines:

- What operational questions must be answered by testing? In OT&E terms, these are called Critical Operational Issues (COIs) and are usually derived from the requirements documentation.
- What must be measured in order to answer the operational questions? In OT&E terms, these are called Measures of Effectiveness/Suitability/Performance (MOE, MOS, and MOPs).
- What specific test data must be collected from those measurements (i.e., test data elements)?
- Under what conditions must the measurements be made and the data collected? (Example: when measuring a response time, a condition might be that the system is under a realistic or stressed load.)

With the above information in hand, design a test regimen to generate the data elements needed to perform the evaluation. It is possible that this test regimen will consist of a compilation vendor-provided test data, developmental test events, and operational test events. In general, the above process applies to all acquisitions with varying levels of rigor applied. For Agile Development programs, however, the operational questions are normally derived from the User Stories targeted for each

140

release, vice an overarching requirements document. For additional information on OT&E, refer to the JITC Operational Test and Evaluation Guidebook, Version 1.2, January 2011.

Joint Interoperability Certification is required to inform decision makers a capability, system, or service has met the requirements identified its NR KPP. The NR KPP is one of six mandatory Key Performance Parameters (KPPs) and is required for all program increments (Joint Capabilities Integration and Development System (JCIDS) Manual, 19 Jan 2012, Para 3, Page B-A-2). All programs designated by Joint Staff (JS) as having joint interoperability requirements will be evaluated by Joint Interoperability Test Command (JITC) for Joint Interoperability Certification. JITC will evaluate joint interoperability of Information Technology (IT) and National Security Systems (NSS) based on their respective JS-certified NR KPP. A system's NR KPP provides measurable and testable effectiveness and performance requirements for the three NR KPP attributes:

- Support Military Operations: This attribute specifies which military operations (e.g., missions or mission threads) a system supports and the operational context for its use.
- Entered and be Managed on the Network: This attribute specifies which network(s) the IT must connect to, the performance requirements for those connections, and the network and IT service management tasks it must support in for net-centric military operations.
- Effectively Exchange Information: This attribute specifies the information elements produced and consumed by each mission and net-ready operational tasks.

JITC assists the designated PMO and supporting test organization in defining the interoperability data collection requirements and the evaluation strategy to address the NR KPP attributes leveraging:

- The NR KPP and associated architecture data, as well as any additional interoperability-related requirements that are not specified in the NR KPP or architecture products themselves, but can be derived from interface specifications or found in other parts of the requirements documents.
- Mission related data using JMTs, if provided,
- Data from DT&E, OT&E, acceptance testing, exercise venues, or other demonstrations, consistent with any approved TES or TEMP, or other interoperability data collection requirements, on technical and operational effectiveness of information exchanges over interfaces from those test events or exercises.

The PMO integrates the interoperability data collection and evaluation strategy into the overall acquisition test, evaluation, and development processes, and the joint interoperability certification is then issued, based on the evaluation results, for each increment of a system. All joint interoperability requirements for a given increment shall be used for evaluation and reporting the status, not just those requirements implemented. If requirements for the system were not delineated by increment (phase, spiral, block, etc.) in the Joint Staff certified NR KPP, all requirements will apply to the current increment. Changing the increment or criticality of a requirement is a modification to the requirements

141

that may require Joint Staff re-certification. For more information on Joint Interoperability Certification, refer to the JITC NR-KPP Guidebook, FY2010.

Testing of the capability should also evaluate the capability to manage, monitor and control the capability.

Additional Testing references can be located at:

- Defense Acquisition Guidebook Chapter 9, Test & Evaluation
- Service Validation and Testing (SVT) CONOPS, Draft Version 1.0, 22 August 2013
- DoD Test and Evaluation Management Guide, Sixth Edition, December 2012

11 Program Reviews

As a program, project, or related effort progresses through the acquisition lifecycle, it will undergo reviews by decision authorities, boards, or panels. Though the official details of each are captured in DoD and DISA policies, this guide provides the common reviews in DISA. As the acquisition team leader develops and executes their acquisition strategies, coordination with key stakeholders throughout the process is essential. Milestones and decision points are gate reviews for approval to the next acquisition phase, but the acquisition team leader should identify how to best leverage these reviews and related coordination as part of their tailored acquisition model and processes. The focus of DISA reviews should be to ensure that the team has done sufficient thinking to develop the strategies and has sufficient support to succeed. Although some elements like IA are critical, these reviews should not be simply to ensure compliance with policies or extensive checklists. Program documentation to support the review should be provided to reviewers with sufficient lead time to enable them to sufficiently prepare and understand the details of the strategy.

Table 6 lists some of the major reviews of acquisition programs within DISA. Though each organization's use of these reviews may vary, the goal is a more consistent use. They will continue to leverage best practices and lessons learned, while tailoring the reviews (including chair and members) based on the size, scope, complexity, and other factors.

Table 6. Major Reviews of Acquisition Programs Within DISA

Review	Details	For More Information
Milestones	Major reviews for programs using Incremental Development of Defense Business System models. MDA reviews and approves strategies and documents for approval to the next acquisition phase. An Acquisition Decision Memorandum (ADM) documents decision.	DoDI 5000.02
Decision Points	Reviews by Decision Authority of the strategy and documents for approval to the next acquisition phase. These are typically done via an Acquisition	DISAI 610-225-2 CAE Guideline 005

	Review Board.	
Acquisition Review Board (ARB)	CAE-level review of acquisition program, projects, initiatives, and services with DISA leadership and key stakeholders. Reviews strategies and provides guidance, direction, and coordination of strategy execution. ARBs can be decisional for Milestones/Decision Points or informational to keep leadership apprised of status and issues.	DISAI 610-225-2 CAE Guideline 005
NetOps Readiness Review Board (NRRB)	Responsible for assessing Agency efforts to ensure that Service Operations capabilities are implemented within DISA programs, systems, applications, and services. Chaired by DISA's OPS Technical Director.	NRRB Website
Chief Engineers Panel (CEP)	Develops and manages changes to the DISA GIG Convergence Master Plan (DGCMP). Ensures all critical programs, projects, initiatives, and services are technically sound and align with the overall agency technical strategy, as articulated in the DGCMP. Conducts or governs technical oversight activities to include requirements reviews, architecture reviews, systems engineering process reviews, and design reviews.	DISAI 610-225-2
The preceding reviews support decision points, whereas the following reviews are used on an as-needed basis.		
Acquisition Related Independent Review (ARIR) Team	An assessment performed on a program, project, service, initiative, topic, or other acquisition-related matter by impartial team members who are not associated with the effort.	CAE Guideline 008
Deep Dive Review	A briefing that provides an extensive in-depth presentation of a topic to provide DISA seniors with a baseline understanding of the background, status, future plans, issues, and risks.	DISAI 610-225-2 and CAE Guideline 008
Independent Review Team (IRT)	A temporary review team of subject matter experts external to the program. They may be tasked at a key point of the program, when the program is facing high risks, or to target a specific aspect of the program.	DoDI 5000.02 and CAE Guideline 008
Peer Review	A pre-award and post-award review of supply and service contracts valued at less than $1B.	DISAI 610-225-2 and CAE Guideline 008

Program Support Review (PSR)	Informs an MDA and acquisition team of the status of technical planning and management processes by identifying cost, schedule, and performance risks and recommended mitigations. Conducted by cross-functional, cross-organizational teams with OSD involvement for those with OSD MDAs.	DoDI 5000.02 and CAE Guideline 008
Configuration Steering Board (CSB)	Reviews all requirements changes and any significant technical changes for ACAT programs in development that potentially will result in cost and schedule impacts.	DISAI 610-225-2

12 Operations and Supports

All DISA acquisitions will be required to complete a Service Operations Annex, a DISA-unique document developed by the Operations Directorate (OPS) and required by OPS for all new DISA acquisitions. The Service Operations Annex provides an overview for how this service is operated and assured. The Annex describes the service's operational stakeholders, operational capability, and specific roles and responsibilities for executing operational processes and functions.

In the strategy and design phase of a service's lifecycle, this annex serves as a top-level planning document to help ensure that the service is appropriately integrated into DISA's Service Operations processes and functions. This document includes a service description to ensure that operational support planning is founded on an understanding of what capabilities the service will deliver to end-users.

In the transition and operations phase, this annex provides all stakeholders with a concise reference as to how the service operates, and who is responsible for various aspects of operations. In particular, this document addresses service-specific responsibilities for executing the processes/functions of the Defense Information Systems Agency Enterprise Service Management Framework (DESMF) Service Operations domain, and addresses how Command and Control (C2) of the service will be conducted.

This document is effective upon approval by the Project Manager and the Service Operations Manager. After initial approval, this document will be updated as needed throughout the service's lifecycle to serve as an authoritative reference for the conduct of service operations.

During the Operations and Support phase, the capability will be operated using the operational processes defined in the DESMF. Depending on the agreed operational concept documented as part of the Service Operations Framework, the acquisition organization may have enduring responsibilities for providing on-call technical expertise to help resolve escalated operational issues. The acquisition team will execute operations and sustainment activities in accordance with the processes described in the Services Operation Annex.

For additional information on sustainment, reference:

- DISA CAE Guideline 002 – Transitioning to Sustainment Phase
- Defense Acquisition Guidebook Chapter 5, Lifecycle Logistics
- DoD Handbook on Product Support Analysis (MIL-HDBK-502A) 18 Mar 13
- DAU Lifecycle Logistics Community of Practice
- Sustaining Software-Intensive Systems, Software Engineering Institute, May 2006

12.1 Sustainment Acquisitions

Sustaining IT capabilities after delivery must be effectively planned early in the acquisition lifecycle and effectively managed throughout operations. The Lifecycle Sustainment Plan (LCSP) captures the sustainment strategies to include performance requirements, support strategies, contracts, issue identification and resolution, technical refresh, training and help desk, funding, management, personnel, integration, retirement, and more. Sustainment acquisitions may include bug fixes, patches, minor COTS upgrades, and improvements to usability, performance, interoperability, and/or operational supportability. Programs may continue to deploy and integrate subsequent releases of new capabilities until they reach a point (e.g., Full Operational Capability) where it is a purely sustainment activity.

To support a deployment decision, rigorous development and operational testing (ideally integrated) will be executed to assess how well the system meets performance requirements. Following deployment, system performance should be assessed again in the full operational environment. System performance should be regularly monitored throughout its operational life, per established criteria and processes captured in the LCSP. This provides feedback to see if requirements have been fully met, identify and assess system deficiencies, and integrate desired changes to the requirements for a subsequent release or patch.

Actively soliciting and effectively capturing end-user feedback is critical throughout the operation and sustainment phase. This may include face-to-face or virtual collaboration with the users, acquisition teams (particularly systems engineers), development contractors, and other stakeholders. Tracking and reporting on help desk tickets can provide quantitative and qualitative data of system deficiencies.

12.1.1   Technology Refresh

Technology refreshment is essentially a COTS IT component and/or system support strategy to extend system service life by addressing COTS logistics concerns. It is the periodic replacement of COTS components (e.g., processors, displays, computer operating systems) and commercially available software within larger DoD systems to assure continued supportability of that system through an indefinite service life. Technology refreshment extends the service life by staying ahead of the obsolescence curve with cost-effective planned technology upgrades, refreshers, and insertions, based on market research and system performance requirements.

- Technology Upgrades: A change that incorporates the next generation product or product upgrade to an existing technology or component that improves overall system functionality. This refreshment may not require redesign of the next higher assembly and is usually form, fit, and function. This type of change can occur at any time during product life.
- Technology Refreshers: A change that incorporates a new product to avoid product end of life or product obsolescence, or to correct a problem based on user feedback. This refreshment may or may not have form, fit, and function, can occur at any time in the life cycle, and re-certification or certification will be required.
- Technology Insertion: A change that incorporates a new product or function capability, which is the result of industry growth or DoD advanced development. This type of refreshment will not have the same form, fit, and function and may require redesign of the next higher assembly, and re-certification.

At the time a tech refresh/upgrade/insertion is required, the acquisition team should collaborate with the CEC and Enterprise Architects to reach an understanding on the scope, complexity, and risk. As a general rule, technology upgrades do not necessarily require re-entry into the acquisition process, especially if the strategy has already been documented in the LCSP. Technology refreshers may require re-entry into the acquisition cycle post-Decision Point 2, if the refreshment requires testing and recertification. Technology insertion does require re-entry at the initiation phase, especially if the program may need to be re-baselined. A major release that requires a change to the underlying system architecture may require the program to revisit the initiation phase and select a new acquisition model. Technology insertion acquisitions will tailor the acquisition process based on the size, scope, and complexity of the effort.

Technology refresh is required not only to maintain capability, but more importantly to constrain costs. As technology used in solutions and services gets further from the commercial offering, the costs for sustainment continue to increase. The activities and costs for technology refresh need to be built into the program baseline at a level that meets industry standards. Often technology refresh is not sufficiently resourced in order to allocate more funding in the portfolio for capability enhancements. This adds risk, cost, and impacts performance, but because it is difficult to quantify, it is often a target of cuts. Each program/portfolio should have a technology refresh plan that addresses all components, software, hardware, integration, etc. At the portfolio and program level, analysis should be ongoing to monitor technology trends and standard technology refresh cycles. The technology refresh plan should reference that analysis and should demonstrate how the technology refresh meets performance requirements.

12.1.1.1   Contract Recompetes

Recompeting the product or service as contract periods of performance end is another form of technology refresh. As the commercial offerings evolve, there are more opportunities to reduce costs through buying services. Over time the commercial service offerings change, the scope of capability increases, and costs decrease. While recompeting enterprise level services has a potential significant

user impact, it also has potential for significant benefit. These opportunities need to be built into the program baseline with all the appropriate decision points. Typically a recompete is initiated with a review and validation of requirements and an acquisition strategy kickoff. The acquisition strategy for a recompete should include reconsidering the roles and responsibilities of the government and contractor based on updated market research. This includes the range of potential alternatives from government owned and operated, to contractor owned and operated. In addition, it should include reassessing the scope of work, whether to expand the scope of the contract vehicles beyond the portfolio, opportunities to lower costs, and alternatives for partitioning the work to improve competition. Since the procurement cycle can take up to two years for a major contract award, the required activities need to be built into the schedule in order to minimize impact to users and maximize continuity.

12.1.2   Performance Management

As an acquisition enters operations and sustainment, continual performance monitoring is expected. The program or portfolio should have a documented set of performance requirements from multiple perspectives to include operational support for the user, network operations, security, system, service levels, etc. From a DISA perspective, products and services need to meet performance targets and expectations through proactive monitoring, in addition to feedback from users. The intent is to identify potential performance issues and have the opportunity to resolve them before they result in significant impact to customers. Ideally performance is monitored through use of tools that provide summary metrics, alerts and dashboards for rapid identification of potential performance issues. A structured assessment takes all sources of information into account to provide a holistic perspective.

In addition to operational and outcome performance monitoring, it is important to monitor the program/project execution for efficiency and sustainability. Every program and project within the portfolio, needs to have allocated cost, schedule and performance parameters. There should be a structured process for execution review to ensure continued ability to meet requirements with existing resources.

Appendix A: References

The following resources are available to the users of this guidebook to obtain additional information on key processes referenced throughout this guide.

Requirements and User Engagements

- CJCSI 3170.01 – Joint Capabilities Integration and Development System (JCIDS)
- JCIDS Manual

Program Management

- Defense Acquisition Guidebook Chapter 2, Program Strategies
- Defense Acquisition Guidebook Chapter 11, Program Management Activities
- DoDD 5000.01 – The Defense Acquisition System
- DODI 5000.02 – Operation of the Defense Acquisition System
- DAU Introduction to Defense Acquisition Management
- Program Management Community on Acquisition Community Connection
- Risk Management Guide for DoD Acquisition
- Open System Architecture Contract Guidebook for Program Managers

Cost Estimation and Budgeting

- Defense Acquisition Guidebook Chapter 3, Affordability and Life-Cycle Resource Estimates
- Better Buying Power
- Estimating Software Earlier and More Accurately
- Procedures and Schedule for Fiscal Year (FY) 2012-2016 Integrated/Budget Review
- DoD Overview on Cost Analysis Requirements Descriptions (CARDs)
- Cost Guidance from Cost Assessment & Program Evaluation (CAPE)
- Joint Memorandum on Savings Related to "Should Cost"
- Cost Estimating Community on Acquisition Community Connection
- DAG Chapter 3.7 on the Principles for Lifecycle Cost Estimates
- GAO Cost Estimating and Assessment Guide
- DoD Standard Practice, Work Breakdown Structures for Defense Materiel Items

Contracting

- Defense Federal Acquisition Regulation Supplement (DFARS) and Procedures, Guidance, and Information (PGI)
- DoD Contracting Officer Representative (COR) Handbook (DPAP 22 Mar 12)
- OMB Contracting Guidance to Support Modular Development
- Contracting Officer Representative - ACQuipedia
- COR Smartcard
- Contracting Community on Acquisition Community Connection

- Service Acquisition Mall (SAM)
- Defense Procurement and Acquisition Policy, Strategic Sourcing
- Small Business Administration (SBA) Market Research
- Office of Management and Budget (OMB) Memorandum, "Mythbusting' – Addressing Misconceptions to Improve Communication with Industry during the Acquisition Process"

Systems Engineering

- DISA Systems Engineering Reference Manual
- Defense Acquisition Guidebook Chapter 4, Systems Engineering
- MITRE Systems Engineering Guide
- Office of the Deputy Assistant Secretary of Defense (ODASD) Systems Engineering

Test and Evaluation

- Defense Acquisition Guidebook Chapter 9, Test & Evaluation
- JITC NR-KPP Guidebook, FY2010
- JITC Operational Test and Evaluation Guidebook, Version 1.2, January 2011
- Service Validation and Testing (SVT) CONOPS, Draft Version 1.0, 22 August 2013
- DoD Test and Evaluation Management Guide, Sixth Edition, December 2012

Clinger Cohen Act

- Defense Acquisition Guidebook, Chapter 7.8
- DISA Instruction 630-225-9.

Sustainment

- DISA CAE Guideline 002 – Transitioning to Sustainment Phase
- Defense Acquisition Guidebook Chapter 5, Lifecycle Logistics
- DoD Handbook on Product Support Analysis (MIL-HDBK-502A) 18 Mar 13
- DAU Lifecycle Logistics Community of Practice
- Sustaining Software-Intensive Systems, Software Engineering Institute, May 2006

Agile

- Estimating on Agile Projects
- Agile Estimating and Planning
- Agile Requirements Best Practices
- Agile Requirements Change Management
- Agile Requirements Modeling
- Agile Software Requirements: Lean Requirements Practices for Teams, Programs, and the Enterprise
- Test and Evaluation for Agile IT
- Shift Left
- Agile Testing Strategies

149

- Agile Testing Strategies
- Agile Testing: A Practical Guide for Testers and Agile Teams
- Manifesto for Agile Software Development
- MITRE Handbook for Implementing Agile in DoD IT Acquisition
- Software Engineering Institute: Considerations for Using Agile in DoD Acquisition
- Software Engineering Institute: Agile Methods: Selected DoD Management and Acquisition Concerns
- GAO Report 12-681 Effective Practices and Federal Challenges in Applying Agile Methods

Other

- DoDI 8410.03, Network Management policy, section 4 of Enclosure 3
- DISA Enterprise Service Management Framework, Edition 1.0, 4 Sep 12
- Carnegie Mellon Software Engineering Institute presentation on Conducting Effective Pilot Studies, 2004
- CISCO Service Level Management: Best Practices White Paper, 4 October 2005
- Best Practices for Service-Level Management by Forrester Research, December 2004

Appendix B: Glossary

Acquisition Model	A set of acquisition phases, processes, and decision points proactively tailored for multiple IT products and services DISA acquires. These are the starting positions for programs to follow with further tailoring allowed.
Acquisition Program	A directed, funded effort that provides a new, improved, or continuing materiel, weapon or information system, or service capability in response to an approved need. (DoDD 5000.01)
Affordability	A determination that the Lifecycle Cost of an acquisition program is in consonance with the long-range investment.
Business Process Reengineering	A systematic analysis and redesign of an organization or enterprise's business processes to improve value, reduce cycle time, and/or cut costs. Identifies processes to be streamlined, automated, or eliminated, often with the integration of business IT systems.
Cost Estimate	An evaluation and analysis of future costs of hardware or services generally derived by relating historical cost, performance, schedule and technical data of similar items or services. DoD 5000.4-M identifies four major analytical methods or cost estimating techniques used to develop cost estimates for acquisition programs: Analogy; Parametric (Statistical); Engineering (Bottoms Up); and Actual Costs.
Concepts of Operations	A Concept of Operations is narrative of the process to be followed in implementing the system. It defines the roles of the stakeholders involved throughout the process. Ideally it should offer clear methodology to realize the goals and objectives for the system, while not intending to be an implementation or transition plan itself. The Concept of Operations document is usually developed in many different ways, but usually includes: • Statement of the goals and objectives of the system • Strategies, tactics, policies, and constraints affecting the system • Organizations, activities, and interactions among participants and stakeholders • Clear statement of responsibilities and authorities delegated • Specific operational processes for fielding the system • Processes for initiating, developing, maintaining, and retiring the system
Contract Performance Management	Contractor performance Management is an assessments (the process known as "quality assurance") that focuses on outcomes rather than on contractor processes. Focus on insight of the contractor performance, not oversight. Periodic assessment of contractor performance should emphasize clear communication, with the objective of encouraging and maintaining high standards of performance, and it should be consistent with past performance assessments.

Commercial Off-the-Shelf (COTS)	COTS items are commercial items that have been sold, leased, or licensed in substantial quantities in the commercial marketplace and that are offered to the government without modification. COTS items are a subset of commercial items.
Decision Authority (DA)	The designated individual with overall responsibility for a program. The DA shall have the authority to approve entry of an acquisition program into the next phase of the acquisition process and shall be accountable for cost, schedule, and performance reporting to higher authority, including Congressional reporting. (Analogous to MDA in DoDD 5000.01)
Decision Point	A review, similar to an acquisition milestone, where the Decision Authority reviews the program's progress and strategy for approval to the next acquisition phase. This could involve a series of reviews with an Acquisition Review Board as the final event.
Defense Business System	A DoD information system, other than a national security system, including financial systems, mixed systems, financial data feeder systems, and IT and information assurance infrastructure. They support business activities such as acquisition, financial management, logistics, strategic planning and budgeting, installations and environment, and human resource management.
Deployment Decision	A decision point to determine if the capability is approved to be deployed to the warfighters. This review includes the Decision Authority, Requirements Owner, acquisition team, and other key stakeholders.
Enterprise Architecture	An Enterprise Architecture (EA) is a rigorous description of the structure of an enterprise, which comprises enterprise components (business entities), the externally visible properties of those components, and the relationships (e.g. the behavior) between them. EA describes the terminology, the composition of enterprise components, and their relationships with the external environment, and the guiding principles for the requirement (analysis), design, and evolution of an enterprise. This description is comprehensive, including enterprise goals, business process, roles, organizational structures, organizational behaviors, business information, software applications and computer systems.
Enterprise Service	A capability that DISA has acquired to provide the DoD enterprise via the DISA Service Catalog. This has been designed to scale for broad adoption and marketed to the enterprise.
Government Off-the-Shelf (GOTS)	Government Off-the-Shelf (GOTS) is a commonly used term for NDIs that are Government-unique items in use by a Federal agency, a State or local government, or a foreign government with which the United States has a mutual defense cooperation agreement.
IA (Information Assurance)	Measures that protect and defend data/information and information systems by ensuring system availability, integrity, authentication, confidentiality, and

	non-repudiation. This includes providing for restoration of information systems by incorporating protection, detection, and reaction capabilities.
Interoperability	DoD policy for systems, units, or forces to provide data, information, materiel, and service, and accept the same data/information from, other systems, units, or forces; and to use the data, information, materiel, and services to enable them to operate effectively together. This includes both the technical exchange of information and the end-to-end operational effectiveness of that exchanged information as required for mission accomplishment. Interoperability is more than just information exchange; it includes systems, processes, procedures, organizations, and missions over the lifecycle and must be balanced with information assurance.
Key Performance Parameter (KPP)	Attributes or characteristics of a system that are considered critical or essential to the development of an effective military capability. A KPP normally has a threshold, representing the required value, and an objective, representing the desired value.
Market Research	A continuous process for gathering data on product characteristics, suppliers' capabilities, and the business practices/trends that surround them -- plus the analysis of that data to make smart acquisition decisions.
Non-Developmental Items	Any previously developed item of supply used exclusively for governmental purposes by a federal agency, a state or local government, or a foreign government with which the United States has a mutual defense cooperation agreement, or any item that requires only minor modification or modifications of a type customarily available in the commercial marketplace in order to meet the requirements of the procuring department or agency
Pilot	The first or initial phase or issuance of a model, system, or item used as a control to test a proposal.
Project	A planned undertaking, independent of a program, having a finite beginning and ending that involves definition, development, production, and logistics support of an IT system(s). A project may be a technology insertion initiative, internal process improvement, technology demonstration, or stand-alone effort.
Project Manager / Project Lead	Same as Program Manager, but for a project. Project Managers and Project Leaders are interchangeable terms within this guidebook.
Program	A directed, funded effort that provides a new, improved, or continuing materiel, weapon or information system, or service capability in response to an approved need. DISA programs typically follow the standard DoD acquisition lifecycle and DoDI 5000.02.
Program Charter	A document that captures the acquisition team's purpose, expectations, responsibilities, planned resources, and outcomes. The charter is often

DISA

	developed by the acquisition team with guidance and direction from the Decision Authority and Requirements Owner.
Program Manager (PM)	The designated individual with responsibility for and authority to accomplish program objectives for development, production, and sustainment to meet the user's operational needs. The PM shall be accountable for credible cost, schedule, and performance reporting to the DA. (DoDD 5000.01)
Prototype	An original or model on which a later system/item is formed or based. Early prototypes may be built and evaluated during the Technology Development Phase, or later in the Engineering and Manufacturing Development phase, or is the result of a Joint Capability Technology Demonstration (JCTD) or Advanced Technology Demonstration (ATD), and tested prior to Milestone C decision. Selected prototyping may continue after Milestone C, as required, to identify and resolve specific design or manufacturing risks, or in support of Evolutionary Acquisition (EA).
Requirements Owner	The individual or group that is responsible for defining, prioritizing, and validating the requirements.
Risk Management Assessment	Risk assessment is a step in a risk management procedure. Risk assessment is the determination of quantitative or qualitative value of risk related to a concrete situation and a recognized threat (also called hazard). Quantitative risk assessment requires calculations of two components of risk: R, the magnitude of the potential loss L, and the probability p, that the loss will occur. In all types of engineering of complex systems sophisticated risk assessments are often made within Safety engineering and Reliability engineering when it concerns threats to life, environment or machine functioning.
Service Available to the Enterprise	A capability DISA developed or acquired for its own use that other organizations have expressed interest in using. DISA provides the capability to the other organization, often for a fee for use. This capability was not designed for or marketed to the DoD enterprise.
Should Cost	A management tool to control costs throughout the program's lifecycle. Should cost targets are below program and independent cost estimates. They are challenges to drive affordability and incentivize industry to eliminate non-value added elements.
Technical Baseline	The description, design, and decomposition of a systems hardware, software, and sub-system integration. Includes system and functional descriptions, key performance parameters, enterprise architectures, interfaces, standards, technology maturity, and evolution strategy.
Tradeoff Analysis	The process of evaluating and selecting among features / functions / performance, operations and support, acquisition strategy approaches, and

	life-cycle funding alternatives with the intent of achieving desired capabilities, performance, sustainment, and mission effectiveness within cost and schedule objectives. Tradeoff analysis compares relative value of parameters in order to achieve a more favorable overall system result. Tradeoff analysis can also consider less than desired performance, showing the impact to military utility, in the interest of maintaining affordability.
Will Cost	The cost estimate performed by the acquisition team or independent group. This is the baseline that a cost target is measured against.

For additional information, see DAU's Glossary of Defense Acquisition Acronyms and Terms.

Appendix C: DoD 5000 Documentation Compliance Matrix

Documents required by Statute for Models 1, 2, 4, 5, 6, and 8.

SYSTEM ACQUISITION FRAMEWORK LIST OF ACAT IA DOCUMENTS (50)	Model 1 (Agile)	Model 2 (Increment al)	Model 4 (IT Commoditi es)	Model 5 (Integ. COTS/ GOTS)	Model 6 (Enterprise Services)	Model 8 (Managed IT Service)	Notes R= Required S= Streamlined/Combined with other Documentation A=As Applicable
DOCUMENTS REQUIRED BY STATUTE (15)							
Acquisition Information Assurance Strategy	S	S	S	S	S	S	Statutory for all IT including NSS. Appendix to the Program Protection Plan (PPP).
Analysis of Alternatives (AoA)	A	A	A	A	A	A	Required for MAIS and AIS programs. This AoA requirement has been tailored into the "Alternatives Analysis" process, which takes place at the Initiation Phase for all acquisitions.
Assessment and Certification of a Critical Change to the Defense Committees	A	A	A	A	A	A	Required for MAIS.
Bandwidth Requirements Review	A	A	A	A	A	A	**Included in Draft DoDI 5000.02. Required for MAIS.**
Benefit Analysis and Determination	A	A	A	A	A	A	Required only for MAIS, ACAT III, and consolidation/bundling acquisitions. Part of the AS.
Beyond Low-Rate Initial Production (LRIP) Report	A	A	A	A	A		Required only for OSD T&E oversight programs.

Appendix C: DoD 5000 Documentation Compliance Matrix

DISA IT Acquisition Guidebook

Business Process Reengineering	S	S	S	S	S	Included in Draft DoDI 5000.02. Required for programs that acquire IT. Part of the AS.
Clinger-Cohen Act (CCA) Compliance	R	R	R	R	R	Required for all IT, including NSS.
Competition Analysis	A	A	A	A	A	Required for MAIS. Competition analysis is summarized in the AS.
Consideration of Technology Issues	A		A	A		Required for MAIS.
Cooperative Opportunities	A		A	A		Required for MAIS and ACAT III.
Core Logistics Analysis/Source of Repair Analysis	A		A	A		Required for MAIS. *Required only for ACAT III in Draft DoDI 5000.02.*
Defense Business Systems Management	A		A	A		Required for MAIS.
Economic Analysis (EA)	A		A	A		Required for MAIS. May be combined with AoA at MS A.
Frequency Allocation Application (DD Form 1494)						Required for MAIS and ACAT III. Statutory for all systems/equipment that use the EM spectrum while operating in the U.S. and its possessions.
Independent Cost Estimates (ICE)	A	A	A	A	A	Required for MAIS.
Information Assurance Strategy	S	S	S	S	S	Included in Draft DoDI 5000.02. Required for all IT programs including NSS. Appendix to PPP.
MAIS Annual Report to Congress	A	A	A	A		Required for MAIS.
MAIS Quarterly Report	A	A	A	A		Required for MAIS.
Market Research	S	S	S	S	S	This requirement has been streamlined. Market research is scoped based on size and complexity of acquisition and is summarized in the AS.

157

VERSION 1.0

Appendix C: DoD 5000 Documentation Compliance Matrix

Document						(Model 7)	Description
Military Equipment Valuation	A	A	A	A	A	A	Required only for MDAP/MAIS and when a deliverable end items meet the requirements for capitalization.
Notice of MAIS Cancellation or Significant Reduction in Scope	A	A	A	A	A		Required for MAIS.
Notification of a Significant Change to the Defense Committees	A	A	A	A	A		Required for MAIS.
Post Implement Review Plan	S	S	S	S			Required for MAIS and ACAT III. Post IOC Reviews. Strategy is described in the LCSP.
Program Deviation Report	A	A	A	A			Required for MAIS immediately upon a program deviation.
Programmatic Environment, Safety, and Occupational Health Evaluation (PESHE)	S	S	S	S		S	Required for all acquisitions. Strategy is described in the AS and LCSP.
Technical Data Rights Strategy	S	S	S	S		S	For ACAT I programs, strategy must be submitted prior to each milestone review as part of the Acquisition Strategy. For all other acquisitions, the strategy should be included in the AS and LCSP.

*Capabilities under Model 7 are initially acquired via another model or legacy system; as a result, there are no DoD 5000 required documents referenced for this model.

**Grey highlighted boxes identify new requirements that are in draft DoDI 5000.02 (currently out for comment).

Appendix C: DoD 5000 Documentation Compliance Matrix

Documents required by regulation for Models 1, 2, 4, 5, 6, and 8.

SYSTEM ACQUISITION FRAMEWORK LIST OF ACAT IA DOCUMENTS (50) DOCUMENTS REQUIRED BY REGULATION (35)	Model 1 (Agile)	Model 2 (Incremental)	Model 4 (IT Commodities)	Model 5 (Integ. COTS/GOTS)	Model 6 (Enterprise Services)	Model 8 (Managed IT Service)	Notes R= Required S= Streamlined/Combined with other Documentation A=As Applicable
Acquisition Decision Memorandum (ADM)	A	A		A	A		Required for MAIS, ACAT III. Reviewed and tracked by AT&L.
Acquisition Program Baseline (APB)	A	A	A	A	A	A	Required at program initiation for ACAT programs. Updated as necessary.
Acquisition Strategy	S	S	S	S	S	S	Required for all acquisitions.
Affordability Assessment	S	S	S	S	S	S	Required for all acquisitions. Assessment summarized in the AS.
Analysis of Alternatives (AoA) Study Guidance	A	A		A	A		Required for MAIS, ACAT II & III. DCAPE approves.
Analysis of Alternatives (AoA) Study Plan	A	A		A	A		Required for MAIS, ACAT II & III.
Capability Development Document (CDD)	A	A		A	A		Required for ACAT Programs. JCIDS Requirement.
Capability Production Document (CPD)	A	A		A	A		Required for ACAT Programs, pre-production.
Cost Analysis Requirements Description (CARD)	A	A		A	A		Required for MAIS and when ICE or EA required.
Corrosion Prevention Control Plan	A	A		A	A		Required for MAIS only. *Not required for MAIS in Draft DoDI 5000.02.*
Defense Acquisition Executive Summary	A	A		A	A		Required for MAIS.

DoD Component Cost Estimate	A	A	A	A	A	Mandatory for MAIS as required by CAE and MDAP. *Required for MAIS when EA is required per DoDI 5000.02 Draft.*
Exit Criteria	A	A	A	A	A	Required for MAIS and ACAT III. Documented in ADM.
Information Operations Capstone Threat Assessment	A	A	A	A		ACAT-IA and IAS programs on DOT&E Oversight List use the DIA-validated assessment (Intel/Threat Analysis).
Information Support Plan (ISP)	S	S	S	S	S	Required for all ACAT programs connecting to IT or NSS programs. Strategy is addressed in the AS.
IT and NSS Joint Interoperability Test Certification	R	R	R	R	R	Required for all IT including NSS.
Initial Capabilities Document (ICD)	A	A	A	A	A	Required for MAIS and ACAT III.
Intellectual Property Strategy	A	A	A	A	A	Included in Draft DoDI 5000.02. Required for MAIS and ACAT III. Part of AS.
Item Unique Identification (IUID) Implementation Plan	A	A	A	A		Used on tangible property, including new equipment, major modifications, and re-procurement of equipment and spares. Qualifying items per (DFARS) 211.274-2.
Joint Assessment						Required for space programs.
Joint Interoperability Test Certification	R	R	R	R	R	Required for IT, including NSS.
Life-Cycle Signature Support Plan	A	A	A	A		Required for Signature dependent technology programs
Life-Cycle Sustainment Plan (LCSP)	S	S	S	S	S	Required for all programs. Document is streamlined and combines information from other required documents.
Net-Centric Data Strategy	A	A	A	A	A	Required for DoD enterprise acquisitions. Strategy is described in the AS.
Operational Test Agency Report of Operational Test and						Required for MAIS and ACAT III.

Appendix C: DoD 5000 Documentation Compliance Matrix

Evaluation Results						
Operational Test Plan	A	A	A	A		Required for MAIS.
Orbital Debris Mitigation Risk Report	A	A	A	A		Required for space programs.
Post-System Design Review Report	A	A	A	A		Required for space programs.
Preliminary Design Review (PDR) Report	R	R	R	R		Required for programs that require development. Document is scoped based on size and complexity of the acquisition.
Program Protection Plan (PPP)	A	A	A	A	A	Required for programs with critical program info. Can be combined into AS.
Request for Proposal (RFP)	R	R	R	R	R	Required for new acquisitions.
Should Cost Target	**R**	**R**	**R**	**R**	**R**	**Included in Draft DoDI 5000.02. Required for all acquisitions.**
Small Business Innovation Research (SBIR) Technologies Consideration	S	S	S	S	S	Required for all acquisitions. Addressed in the AS.
Spectrum Supportability Determination	A	A	A	A	A	Required for Systems using electromagnetic spectrum. Included in the AS and LCSP.
Systems Engineering Plan (SEP)	A	A	A	A		Required for ACAT programs. Systems engineering strategy is addressed in the AS.
Systems Engineering Trade-Off Analysis	**A**	**A**	**A**	**A**	**A**	**Included in Draft DoDI 5000.02. Required for MAIS and ACAT III.**
System Threat Assessment Report (STAR)	A	A	A	A		Required for MAIS and ACAT III programs. Use the DIA Info Ops Capstone Threat Assessment
Technical Data Rights Strategy	S	S	S	S	S	Required for all IT. Technical data strategy addressed in the AS and LCSP.
Technology Development Strategy (TDS)	A	A	A	A	A	Required for all technology development acquisitions. Strategy can be combined with the AS.

Appendix C: DoD 5000 Documentation Compliance Matrix

Technology Readiness Assessment	S	S		S	S	Required for all technology development acquisitions. Assessment is summarized in the AS.
Test and Evaluation Master Plan (TEMP)	S	S		S	S	Required for all acquisitions that require testing. Test strategy can be combined with the AS.
Test and Evaluation Strategy (TES)	S	S	S	S	S	Required for all acquisitions that require testing. Test strategy can be combined with the AS.
Waveform Development or Modification Application	A	A	A	A	A	S	Applicable to development of new or modified waveforms

*Capabilities under Model 7 are initially acquired via another model or legacy system; as a result, there are no DoD 5000 required documents referenced for this model.

**Grey highlighted boxes identify new requirements that are in draft DoDI 5000.02 (currently out for comment).

Documents required for Model 3, Defense Business Systems, according to BCL.

DEFENSE BUSINESS SYSTEM ACQUISITION LIST OF ACAT IA REQUIRED DOCUMENTS	Model 3 (Defense Business Systems)	Notes R= Required S= Required but Streamlined/Combined with other Documentation A=As Applicable
Business Case	S	Required for MAIS. Programs below IA threshold coordinate at the component level.
Analysis of Alternatives	A	Required for MAIS. Summarized in the Business Case.
Cost Estimate	A	Required for MAIS. Agency conducts cost estimate, reviewed by DCAPE. For ACAT IAM, If USD(AT&L) is MDA and critical change occurs, DCPAE

Appendix C: DoD 5000 Documentation Compliance Matrix

Document		Notes
		conducts an ICE.
Economic Analysis	A	Required for MAIS. Summarized in the Business Case.
Market Research	S	Required for DBS.
Acquisition Approach	S	Required for DBS.
Technical Data Rights Strategy	S	Summarized in the Business Case.
Information Support Plan	S	Summarized in the Business Case.
Lifecycle Sustainment Plan (LCSP)	S	Summarized in the Business Case.
Systems Engineering Plan (SEP)	S	Summarized in the Business Case.
Technology Development Strategy (TDS)	S	Required for all IT. Summarized in the Business Case.
Test Plan	S	Summarized in the Business Case. May integrate with SEP as appropriate.
Acquisition Decision Memorandum (ADM)	A	Required for MAIS. Reviewed and tracked by AT&L.
Acquisition Information Assurance Strategy	S	Required for all IT including NSS. Appendix to the PPP.
Acquisition Program Baseline (APB)	A	Required for MAIS. Includes KPPs from Business Case.
Analysis of Alternatives (AoA) Study Guidance	A	Required for MAIS & ACAT III. DCAPE approves.
Analysis of Alternatives (AoA) Study Plan	A	Required for MAIS & ACAT III.
Business Process Reengineering	S	Required for DBS. Precursor to AoA. Process described in Business Case.
Component Acquisition Executive (CAE) Compliance Memorandum	R	Required for DBS.

Appendix C: DoD 5000 Documentation Compliance Matrix

Document		Requirement
Certification of Compliance to Title 10 USC 2222	A	Required for programs >$1 million over the current FYDP. Included as part of the CAE Compliance Memorandum
Clinger-Cohen Act (CCA) Compliance	R	Required for all IT including NSS.
Cost Analysis Requirements Description (CARD)	A	Required for MAIS and when ICE or EA required. Do not duplicate info in Business Case, reference as appropriate.
Enterprise Risk Assessment Methodology (ERAM) Assessment	A	Required for MAIS. DBS below MAIS must establish procedures to assess risk.
Independent Cost Estimate (ICE)	A	ICE conducted by DCAPE required for MAIS programs if USD(AT&L) is MDA. If MDA is other than USD(AT&L), Agency conducts cost estimate and review by DCAPE.
Independent Risk Assessment	**R**	**Required for DBS in Draft of DoDI 5000.02.**
Information Assurance Strategy	**S**	**Included in Draft DoDI 5000.02. Required for all IT programs including NSS. Summarized in Business Case.**
IT & NSS Joint Interoperability Test Certification (IT & NSS JITC)	R	Required for all IT, including NSS.
Intellectual Property Strategy	**A**	**Included in Draft DoDI 5000.02. Required for MAIS and ACAT III. Summarized in Business Case.**
Operational Test Agency Report of OT&E Results	A	Required for OSD OT&E oversight programs only.
Operational Test Plan	A	Required for OSD OT&E oversight programs only.
Post-Implementation Review (PIR)	S	Required for DBS. The IRB close out review is the PIR. PIR planning documented in Business Case.

Appendix C: DoD 5000 Documentation Compliance Matrix

Document	Code	Notes
Program Charter	R	Required for DBS.
Program Deviation Report	A	Required for DBS immediately upon a program deviation.
Programmatic Environment, Safety, and Occupational Health Evaluation (PESHE)	S	Required for DBS. The Acquisition Approach must contain a summary of the PESHE.
Spectrum Supportability Determination and Application for Equipment Frequency Allocation (DD Form 1494)	A	Generally does not apply to DBS.
Program Protection Plan	A	Required for programs with critical program information.
Problem Statement	S	Required for DBS in lieu of the JCIDS process and JCIDS documentation for DBS, and may support other analyses.
Request for Proposal (RFP)	R	Required for DBS.

Documents required for Model 9, Acquisition of Services, according to DoD 5000.

SERVICES ACQUISITION LIST OF REQUIRED DOCUMENTS (All Service Acquisitions)	Model 9 (Acquisition of Services)	Notes R= Required S= Required but Streamlined/Combined with other Documentation A=As Applicable
Requirements Development		
Market Research	S	Include in Acquisition Strategy
Cost Estimate	R	Cost estimate for total planned acquisition lifecycle
Metrics	A	Include in QASP/SLAs
Acquisition Approach		
Milestones	S	Summarized in the Acquisition Plan

Appendix C: DoD 5000 Documentation Compliance Matrix

Cost Estimate	S	Summarized in the Acquisition Plan
Technical, Business, Management Considerations	S	Summarized in the Acquisition Plan
Competition Expectations	S	Summarized in the Acquisition Plan
Socio-economic Considerations	S	Summarized in the Acquisition Plan
Source Selection Plan	R	For Competitive Acquisitions
Required Deviations or Waivers	A	Document in J&A or as required by local policy
Determination of Inherently Governmental Functions	S	Summarized in the Acquisition Plan
Lease/Purchase Analysis	A	If required by OMB Circular A-94, Section 13
Solicitation and Contract Award		
Type of Business Arrangements Anticipated	S	Summarized in the Acquisition Plan
Duration of Business Arrangement	S	Base plus all option periods. Summarized in the Acquisition Plan
Pricing Arrangements/Incentives	S	Summarized in the Acquisition Plan
Risk Management	R	Assessment of current and potential technical, cost, schedule, and performance risks and mitigation plan
Contract Tracking & Oversight	R	Management approach following contract award, QASP or written oversight plans and responsibilities, and tracking procedures or processes used to monitor contract performance
Performance Evaluation	R	Plan for evaluating whether the metrics and any other measures identified to guide the acquisition have been achieved
Title 40/CCA Compliance (Service Acquisitions > $500M)		
1. Make a determination that the acquisition supports core, priority functions of the Department. [2]	R	ICD Approval
2. Establish outcome-based performance measures linked to strategic goals. [2,3]	R	ICD, CDD, CPD and APB approval
3. Redesign the processes that the system supports to reduce costs, improve effectiveness and maximize the use of COTS technology. [2,3]	R	Approval of the ICD, Concept of Operations, AoA, CDD, and CPD

Appendix C: DoD 5000 Documentation Compliance Matrix

4. Determine that no Private Sector or Government source can better support the function. [4]	R	Acquisition Strategy, AoA
5. Conduct an analysis of alternatives. [3,4]	R	AoA
6. Conduct an economic analysis that includes a calculation of the return on investment; or for non-AIS programs, conduct a Life-Cycle Cost Estimate (LCCE). [3,4]	R	Program LCCE, Program Economic Analysis for MAIS
7. Develop clearly established measures and accountability for program progress.	R	Acquisition Strategy, APB
8. Ensure that the acquisition is consistent with the DoD Information Networks (DODIN) policies and architecture, to include relevant standards.	R	APB (Net-Ready KPP), ISP (Information Exchange Requirements)
9. Ensure that the program has an information assurance strategy that is consistent with DoD policies, standards and architectures, to include relevant standards. [3]	R	Acquisition Information Assurance Strategy
10. Ensure, to the maximum extent practicable, (1) modular contracting has been used, and (2) the program is being implemented in phased, successive increments, each of which meets part of the mission need and delivers measurable benefit, independent of future increments.	R	Acquisition Strategy
11. Register Mission-Critical and Mission-Essential systems with the DoD CIO. [3,5]	R	DoD

1. The system documents/information cited are examples of the most likely but not the only references for the required information. If other references are more appropriate, they may be used in addition to or instead of those cited. Include page(s) and paragraph(s), where appropriate.

2. These requirements are presumed to be satisfied for Weapons Systems with embedded IT and for Command and

Control Systems that are not themselves IT systems.

VERSION 1.0

3. These actions are also required to comply with section 811 of Reference (ag).

4. For NSS, these requirements apply to the extent practicable (section 11103 of Reference (v))

5. Definitions:

Mission-Critical Information System. A system that meets the definitions of "information system" and "national security system" in the CCA (Reference (v)), the loss of which would cause the stoppage of warfighter operations or direct mission support of warfighter operations. (The designation of mission critical shall be made by a Component Head, a Combatant Commander, or their designee. A financial management IT system shall be considered a mission-critical IT system as defined by the Under Secretary of Defense (Comptroller) (USD(C)).) A "Mission-Critical Information Technology System" has the same meaning as a "Mission-Critical Information System."

Mission-Essential Information System. A system that meets the definition of "information system" in Reference (v), that the acquiring Component Head or designee determines is basic and necessary for the accomplishment of the organizational mission. (The designation of mission-essential shall be made by a Component Head, a Combatant Commander, or their designee. A financial management IT system shall be considered a mission-essential IT system as defined by the USD(C).) A "Mission-Essential Information Technology System" has the same meaning as a "Mission-Essential Information System."